AMA RESEARCH STUDY 105

MANAGING THE MAJOR SALE

William H. Kaven

AMERICAN MANAGEMENT ASSOCIATION, INC.

This Research Study has been distributed without charge to AMA members enrolled in the Marketing Division.

International standard book number: 0–8144–3105–4
Library of Congress catalog card number: 71–143265

Contents

1. Overview and Major Conclusions

While the processes involved in the management of the usual day-to-day commercial transactions are widely understood, there has been little exploration into the management of special or major sales. This study, based on 19 in-depth interviews in a variety of American and Canadian business organizations, attempts to discover what companies do in making major sales happen.

In this study major sales have been defined as (1) an expensive single purchase such as a computer installation, a logging system, or an industrial site or (2) a close relationship in which the seller serves the buyer on a continuing basis as a major source of services, materials, or goods, such as selling a group insurance plan for a company's employees, steel to an auto plant, or ice cream to a food chain.

All 19 companies had well-defined, highly developed systems for making regular sales, but there were generally far less formalized procedures for major sales. In fact, there was virtually no written material on the topic.

At the onset of the interview at nearly every company, it became apparent that a great number and variety of people were involved in bringing the major sale to fruition. Frequently, those who were involved in the management of large sales were not even officially labeled salesmen. Titles included president, vice-president, district manager, project supervisor, systems engineer, marketing specialist, industrial development engineer, sales engineer—any title necessary to get the job done. One company, The Macke Company, even has a slogan, "EMMAS—Every Macke Man a Salesman."

In many areas of business, men labeled salesmen never wrote an order; they merely maintained contact and generally served to improve relations with customers.

What was being sold generally in major sales was not something off the shelf but a proposition tailored to the particular needs of the prospect. This was true even in consumer goods, where the sales program rather than the can of soup or quart of ice cream was the major sale.

All the companies faced three common selling problems in producing their major sales: (1) The special design required research into the clients' problems, needs, capabilities, and expectations; (2) the seller had to call on his own resources to develop the right design, to put together an effective sales proposal, and to convince a whole committee of practical-minded executives of the value of the proposal; and (3) after the agreement the seller had to continue to maintain contact to see the system installed properly and functioning effectively.

The magnitude of the task in producing major sales was virtually overwhelming. When one considers such major inputs as geographical distance, political and legal complications, estimates and proposals, product research, and backup and service personnel and systems, the effort, coordination, drive, and patience required are almost limitless. One sales executive described a series of problems that over three years included many political obstacles in both government and business circles that would discourage the average businessman. Opposition to his efforts included an unveiled threat of loss of patronage to his prospects by a major corporation.

The companies studied were chosen for their dissimilarity so as to obtain a broad cross section of products, industries, and management styles. On page 9 is a breakdown of the sample by industry and product or service.

CONCLUSIONS

The following four conclusions may be drawn from this study.

1. *Sales-sequence pattern.* First, there is a general pattern, or a sequence of ten steps, involved in the completion of a major sale.

Chapter 2: Consumer Goods	*Product*
Hendrie's Inc.	Ice cream
Catelli–Five Roses	Canned food
Chapter 3: Installations	
A logging systems company	Logging systems
Canadian Pacific	Industrial sites
A computer manufacturer	Computers
Acme Visible Records, Inc.	Record systems
Canadian General Electric Company Limited	Paper mill drive systems
Chapter 4: Services	
Air Survey Corporation	Photogrammetry
A telephone company	Telephone communications
Canadian Pacific	Freight and physical distribution
The Lincoln National Life Insurance Company	Group insurance
The Macke Company	Industrial feeding
D. H. Overmyer Company, Inc.	Public warehousing
Chapter 5: Materials	
Du Pont of Canada Limited	Synthetic fibers
An aluminum company	Aluminum
A steel company	Steel
The Ogilvie Flour Mills Company, Limited	
Industrial Grain Products Limited	Starches and chemicals
Food Service Division	Processed eggs
Ogilvie Bakery and Industrial Foods	Bakery flour

- Preintelligence: The salesman obtains information about the prospect and his needs.
- Contact: The salesman contacts the prospect company, seeking out the highest-ranking decision maker in that area, frequently the chief executive officer. The executive may then send the salesman on down to the appropriate person, or discuss the matter himself.
- Obtain permission to survey: The salesman requests permission to survey the prospect company to find problems that the salesman's company can solve.
- Perform the survey.
- Review own resources: The salesman calls on the backup resources available to him both from within and from without his company.
- Tailor sales proposal: The salesman, working with his backup people, puts together a sales proposal to be presented to the prospect.

- Present proposal: The salesman presents his sales proposal to the prospect. The nature of the proposal meeting, who is to be present from the seller and the prospect, the style of proposal, and the objective of the meeting itself vary widely. The ultimate objective, of course, is to obtain the prospect's approval and thus a major sale.
- Obtain prospect approval.
- Seller fulfills agreement.
- Maintenance selling: After the sale is consummated and the agreement fulfilled, the salesman maintains close contact with the customer. He is in effect constantly engaging in preintelligence, so he is prepared to move quickly and easily into further major sales with the same customer.

Of course, there is a recycling of these procedures for each new major sale.

2. *Maintenance selling.* The second major conclusion evolves from the last step of this sales sequence. In effect, maintenance selling following a major sale is the same process as "preintelligence." The functions of maintenance selling in managing major sales can be described as follows.

- *Opening-wedge function.* The regular salesman, in contacting his regular customers and prospects, frequently sells nothing at all, is little involved in his company's decision-making function, receives far more direction than he gives, often calls on no one but lower-echelon personnel on his sales route, and is frequently excluded from upper-echelon entertainment. Yet, through his routine efforts of maintaining viable relationships with his clientele, and by keeping an eye out for opportunities for potential sales in the marketplace, the salesman serves as the opening wedge for new major sales.
- *Intelligence function.* The regular salesman is the vital link in the communication chain between seller and customer or prospective customer. His standard duties include keeping the buyers informed on prices, packing, deliveries, developments, changes, and advantageous buys and promotions.

Two intelligence activities in particular are of very special value to his company. First, he gathers important information from his contacts—for example, plans for new purchases, new plants, new products, new sales and production programs. Second, the salesman's observations of the marketplace in relation to his customers and competitors guide his company in developing marketing strategies and competitive tactics.

- *Selling function.* The salesman is engaged primarily in obtaining orders and reorders and secondarily in insuring that what he sells stays sold. This second function forms a base for making major sales. It is promotion and goodwill advertising; it is an indication of the company's dependability and its interest in serving its customers. And, by eliminating obstacles and frictions that could prevent future sales, it is one way to cement the intercompany relationship.

3. *Who manages the sales effort?* In about 80 percent of the companies studied, the management of the major sale was under the direction of the salesman contacting that account. However, there are a number of factors that will lend a different meaning to this broad statement.

The salesman may not even carry the title "salesman." In his company he might be called a district manager, a project supervisor, a systems engineer, a marketing specialist, a sales engineer, an industrial development engineer, or some other similar title. All such titles ordinarily imply sales as a primary duty. There are, however, some companies in which executives holding primary duties other than sales actually are the sales contact with a particular customer. Such practice has frequently developed because the executive has a long-standing connection with the customer that may go back to his days as a salesman.

The salesman managing the effort on major sales is usually a specialized and well-experienced man who has great knowledge in his field, in his product, in the internal operations of both his own company and his customer's.

The salesman depends a great deal on the support of backup personnel within his company: designers, engineers, marketing experts, financial advisers, and anyone else who can give him special advice. His superior is generally extremely knowledgeable in developing strategy and opening up avenues within the company. The salesman will also call upon special personnel who can add value to the sales effort by contacting a prospective customer. Several years ago the vice-president of a major East Coast food processing company demonstrated his role as a friendly aid to the salesman's effort. He picked up the phone, called the president of a food chain the company wanted to supply, and invited the president and his wife to join him and his wife. in New York City for a weekend of shows. Only a few weeks later, the contract was completed and announced in the trade papers.

The salesman may already have considerable top-echelon support in that his company's executives are already in some contact with the prospect. The executives may have met him at some industry function and established cordial relations.

4. *Bases for variations in sales strategy.* Obviously not all sales strategies are the same. They vary for a number of reasons, but two are especially worth mentioning.

• *Uniqueness or substitutability of what is being sold.* Unique products such as a tract of land, a patented process, a proprietary label, or a special technical ability are sold through a strategy that keys on their uniqueness. Presentation to the prospect is based primarily upon a delineation of the facts.

Substitutable products or services, on the other hand, are sold through strategies carefully designed to consider the human factor more precisely—the person doing the buying. In these companies, the interviews focused on issues that were not prevalent among suppliers of unique products and services, such as how to make a call, what to say or avoid saying, how to design a successful proposal meeting, the importance of entertainment, and the value of status.

One sales executive described a carefully developed plan to close a major contract with a good prospect. The prospect was invited for a company tour and was flown in on the seller's jet. The president of the host company, learning of the prospect's religious background, decided on a soft, friendly approach, which included a small private dinner for a handful of executives from both companies. After dinner the host went for a quiet summer evening stroll with his main guest. The host asked the prospect how he got along with his sons, who were in the business with their father, and then waxed philosophical about his own relations as a young man with his own father—all according to script. As he wound up the stroll with the prospect, he commented that he felt that the prospect really understood him. The prospect replied quietly, "I do understand you. You're telling me that your competitor's stuff is no good and that I should start buying from you."

• *Who is being sold.* Many companies alter the strategy and presentation according to the information needed by the buyer and the questions he will ask to help him make his decision. Presentations may be changed within one prospective company depending on the composition of the group. For example, purchasing agents and divisional managers may raise quite specific questions dealing with performance and price. Presentations to top executives tend toward impressing them with the seller's overall competence. Presentations to engineers would emphasize areas of interest to them.

OBSERVATIONS AND TRENDS

During the interviews with various executives in the companies studied, ten trends came to light, explicitly as well as implicitly. While not to be stated as conclusions, they are worthy of mention here.

1. *Trend to larger sales.* Major sales appear to account for an increasing percentage of total sales dollars in the companies studied. Certainly this trend is apparent where selling to a few chain store organizations is tantamount to regional or national distribution, where one insurance policy can provide protection for thousands of employees, where the contract for one computer installation is more than equal to the lifetime sales record of an adding machine salesman.

The causes of the trend to larger sales are numerous. The major factors are the increased technical complexity of the products offered, increased economic concentration and drive for efficiency, and, subsequently, a larger scale of operations and purchases.

2. *Increased seller interest in buyer's decisions.* As major sales begin to account for a larger portion of the seller's business, he recognizes that the buyer's decision becomes even more vital to his operations and profitability. The impact of gaining the Great Atlantic and Pacific Tea Company as a customer is far greater than gaining the patronage of one corner grocery store.

The consummation of a major sale requires the successful crossing of so many hurdles at such great expense that the seller seeks to reduce the risk of failure. Generally this entails staying close to the buyer so as to gather intelligence during the decision-making period.

The knowledgeable salesman is frequently able to make direct inquiries—"How do we look with your people, Charlie?"—without appearing pushy. At higher echelons the buyer and the seller may meet for a brief word in passing at a directors meeting of a hospital, bank, or community chest. The executive of the prospect company might hint, "Have you been having problems with your drive assemblies?" If pushed for further comments, the buyer would likely fall silent. When the executive of the selling company returns to his office, he calls a meeting to discuss the prospect's concern about his drive assembly and get to the root of the problem. Perhaps some other customer has had such a problem and a competitor has carried the story to the prospect. The sales organization then takes action to dispel the prospect's concern and maintain the possibility of a favorable decision.

3. *Increased buyer–seller interrelationship.* The increased size and complexity of major sales are bringing about a closer relationship between buyer and seller. The need to deliver what is needed by the buyer on schedule is of such great importance to the operation of both the seller and the buyer that their interrelationship can best be described as symbiotic.

Unless buyer and seller in a major sale know each other's operations well, the chance of an interruption in the flow of goods or services is increased, just as is the likelihood of a delay in a vital installation. Several examples serve to illustrate the vital interdependency.

• Major auto makers must discuss, far in advance, production and sales patterns with the railroads that service them so that rail cars can be built and will be ready to haul away automobiles on schedule.

• A major cigarette manufacturer had to take a supplying printing company into its confidence and divulge projected sales figures of various brands, sizes, and packings. Prior to this close relationship, the printer received only last-minute orders that created such chaos that pressmen either were laid off or had to work overtime; some quit as a result.

• Both computer and telephone companies have major account salesmen whose sole responsibility is to take care of the needs of but one account. It is not uncommon for such salesmen to maintain an office in the client's own office area. The same is true of several large food manufacturers that have men assigned to and stationed on the premises of a major food retailer or wholesaler.

• The flow of egg supply between Canada's largest seller and its largest user is so vital that the seller helps the buyer determine his purchases. The buyer closely inspects the conditions of production and the flow of processed eggs through the supplier's plant.

• While it is common for buyers to supply, directly or indirectly, credit information to their suppliers, it is not yet common for the reverse to be true. But more large buyers, in an attempt to insure their incoming supplies, demand credit and financial data from their suppliers in addition to a personal inspection of the premises.

• Some large buyers ask for a computation of their suppliers' bids if they appear too low or too high. It serves no good end to buy from a low bidder only to have him become bankrupt, with the order incomplete.

4. *Political consideration.* There are so many inputs to the purchase decision in the client company that the seller must be keenly aware of its internal politics and subtleties if he is to consummate the sale. In one company, for example, great care was taken to avoid appearing to exert pressure or going over a decision maker's head. Yet on the other hand the sellers did not wish to slight the top executives. Management shuffles were frequently studied to discern whether they boded good or ill for the seller. The salesman always kept open his contacts, old and new, regardless of rank—just in case.

5. *The top executive's role in closing major sales.* In some companies top executives, who already have other regular duties, are called in by the marketing and sales departments to help close large sales. Such efforts may involve high-level entertainment such as golf, hunting, fishing, spectator sports, or excellent meals. These efforts may also include the renewal of an old friendship or the lending of some heavy executive weight to impress the buyer of the importance of the sale. Executive jets are useful and impressive, too. Top executives from all functional areas are subject to such requests if their expertise—official or unofficial—can help bring about a successful sale.

One top executive stated emphatically, however, that none of his fellow executives was involved in helping to produce large orders except in their corporate function as requested: Finance officers helped only to arrange finance; production chiefs solved only production problems, but in no way would they help entertain or convince a prospective customer. In fact, this executive added, he couldn't discuss business with client executives when he met them socially because he had no idea what purchase decisions were pending.

Those top executives who do help to close sales, which is the case in most of the companies studied, are of two minds about what to ask for when entertaining. One group merely entertains, perhaps discusses general business conditions, but does not ask for a specific order, feeling that patronage is implicit in entertainment. Worth noting, however, is the comment of one major sales executive who stated very explicitly, "It is a cardinal sin in this firm not to ask for an order when you have entertained someone. The customer knows why he is there, and expects to be asked."

6. *Sale size and executive involvement.* The larger the transaction relative to company size, the higher the level of executive involved. This obtains generally for both seller and buyer.

7. *The role of personal selling.* Personal selling is certainly still present, alive, and well, but it has undergone several changes in its adaptation to modern major sales techniques: (1) It is less flamboyant and overwhelming than in the days of the drummer. Now major sales are far too complicated and technical, and buyers' decisions far too involved, for one man to bring off with any continuing degree of success. (2) Inspirational selling techniques and daily sales pep rallies have been replaced by solid training in the nature of the product or service being sold. Pep rallies may have helped the shy insurance salesman close the sale of a burial policy to a close relative, but the group insurance policies are bought from the professionally competent. Major sales involve expertise, know-how, and homework before and after each call. (3) Personal selling must now be an adjunct to an already well-planned and well-executed sales strategy. It provides that measure of personal relationship at all levels that gives added reason for the buyer to buy.

8. *Postsale involvement.* The agreement to buy and the completion of installation do not end the close relationship between buyer and seller. Neither party wants it to end, actually. In making his purchase decision, the buyer looks closely at the kind of care he will receive over time. He wants warranties fulfilled and service contracts maintained; in addition he may need long-term financing. The seller wants the postsale involvement, and plans carefully for it. He knows that "sell and run" is no longer acceptable. Postsale involvement gives the seller the advantages of maintenance selling: good intelligence

for new orders, the operating wedge to getting the order, and the insurance that the present sale stays happily sold.

9. *Earnings ceilings.* In many companies there is a ceiling on the earnings of the salesman, imposed by his physical limitations in making calls, preparing proposals, making callbacks, waiting, and traveling. One sales executive frankly stated that his salesmen virtually could not earn more than $15,000 to $17,000 per year. The real need, as the sales executive will understand, was to create products or packages of products that could be sold together to create a higher dollar volume and earnings per call. An additional need, of course, was to lighten the salesman's clerical load to permit him more time in the field.

10. *Patience in major sales.* Of very real importance in managing the large sale is immense patience over long periods of time. Large sales seldom appeared to materialize without prior knowledge.

Long-term relationships between the selling and the buying companies or between key individuals at the two companies helped the sale. As mentioned, long-standing personal friendships between top executives in the selling and the buying companies are not uncommon, or without influence on the sale. These might have begun years earlier when a young salesman was calling upon a young buyer, and continued over time.

2. Consumer Goods

Iɴ consumer goods industries the major sale is defined not as a large single order but as the establishment of an ongoing relationship in which the supplier will serve as a major source to a new retailer for a given product or product line. Food and grocery manufacturers, the supply side of the major segment of the consumer goods industry, provide excellent examples for study. Following a discussion of current challenges in selling to mass retailers, this chapter will explore the major sale in two manufacturing companies in the grocery industry: Hendrie's Inc. and Catelli–Five Roses.

CHALLENGES IN SELLING TO MASS RETAILERS

With the vast improvement in communication and transportation have come the growth of mass-selling, multiple-store operations, increased availability of consumer goods, and increased buyer and consumer market sophistication. Such changes have brought new challenges to the manufacturers of consumer goods.

Limited selling space. Implicit in mass selling is the concept of fewer but larger outlets. This in turn places a tremendous value on each outlet gained or lost. The continued introduction of new products, new sizes, new packing, and new brands makes the shortage of selling space acute. Even though many mass-selling outlets stock as many as eight thousand items—ten times what the corner store stocked in the 1920s—the selling space is very limited.

Increased centralization of the buying function. As the multiple-store concept grows, fewer individual buyers make the decisions for a greater segment of the retail market. It has been estimated that fewer than 100 buyers control the decisions to buy certain new grocery products in outlets representing over 50 percent of U.S. retail grocery sales. Store managers, whether chain or affiliated independent, do little if any buying; they merely possess varying degrees of freedom to accept or reject items from a list already prescreened at a distribution center.

Changes in the sales function. Introducing new products or lines into mass retail outlets requires a combined effort. It is seldom that the regular salesman calling on a buyer for a chain, group, or division can bring a major sale to fruition by himself. If the effort is to be successful, he needs the support of a wide array of people.

Selling to mass retailers requires new sales specialties. The salesman calling upon the individual chain or affiliated store performs a maintenance function—obtaining reorders, keeping buyers advised, and maintaining good relations with the store manager. He is engaged more in institutional selling than in product selling. Many such men never write an order. Introduction of new products or lines is usually accomplished at higher levels in both the selling and the buying companies, although the salesman may be present at these meetings.

As the buying function becomes more centralized and the purchasing division becomes more important to the buyer as well as the seller, the seller must develop his strategy with increasing care. The introduction of a new product or line to a large buyer becomes a high-level activity, a major *tour de force* involving great planning.

Few second chances for poor-performing products. One additional but important point: In consumer goods, unlike other areas studied, the final decision regarding product success rests with the consumer. The test is whether the consumer finds sufficient merit in the product to buy it on a continuing basis. Regardless of the elaborate effort to gain entry onto the buyer's shelves, the product can be delisted and disappear in 30 days. Reentry into the store is far more difficult—if not impossible; the countless products waiting in the wings to come on stage will quickly fill the slot.

Case Studies

The two companies that were studied are from the food industry, primarily because it is America's largest industry and represents by far the major portion of the consumer goods segment. Although both firms sell to somewhat similar spectrums of retailers, their methods of operation are different. Even more dissimilar are their objectives in a major sale.

Hendrie's Inc., Milton, Massachusetts, a New England company dating back to 1885, now comprises four distinct but highly interrelated functional divisions: ice cream: manufacturing and distribution; public cold storage: warehousing and distribution; frozen foods: warehousing and distribution; and new product-service development: marketing and distribution. The company has grown rapidly since 1962 and is now the third largest ice cream producer in New England—just behind Hoods and Sealtest, industry giants.

Catelli–Five Roses is a Canadian-owned grocery company operating across Canada and in the eastern United States. Its product lines are separated into four divisions—canned goods: Habitant and Catelli brands; pickles: Habitant; flour and mixes: Five Roses, Twinkle, Ogilvie; pasta: Catelli. The American division, Catelli–Habitant, Inc. (U.S.A.), produces and sells soups mainly in New England at this stage. The company is a major factor in the Canadian food market and is viewed as a quality manufacturer.

Major Conclusion

The major conclusion to be drawn from these complementary cases is based upon differences rather than similarities between the two companies. Although Hendrie's and Catelli may be selling to the same grocery chain or group, their objectives are, as mentioned, actually quite different. Catelli, on one hand, seeks to get its product listed in the chain or group computer so that the stores will order and reorder as needed from the central warehouse. Hendrie's, on the other hand, seeks to become the store's sole ice cream supplier and to design and manage the store's ice cream marketing program.

The major difference in sales objectives, of course, in no way reflects differences in managerial skills; it derives essentially from the basic difference in the products of the two companies. In addition, perishability has brought about differences in the companies' distribution channels, industry sales practices, and seller–client relationships. Ice cream, being very perishable, is sold by the manufacturer direct to retailers of all sizes and only in trading areas where the product can be delivered in good quality. The ice cream manufacturer is thus able to control conditions literally to the point of sale and insure quality for the consumer. On the other hand, canned soup has a great shelf life and is easily transportable; it is sold direct to only the largest retailers. Other retailers purchase through wholesalers.

Product perishability also determines industry sales practices. Canned soup, requiring relatively little care or special handling, permits retailers to stock several brands with ease. This deprives Catelli–Five Roses of the opportunity to serve as exclusive supplier. Thus the company has little opportunity to effect changes beneficial to it within the stores; it has little opportunity to suggest retail prices, nor can it add new items at will. In effect it can do little within the store to increase the likelihood of being selected by the housewife. The goal of the company—to obtain a listing in the computer and compulsory distribution into the stores—is about the maximum to be achieved for most items in a grocery store.

On the other hand, ice cream manufacturers like Hendrie's have been able to establish a very different sort of relationship. The retailer usually grants an exclusive relationship even though consumer franchise and brand loyalty are not prevalent in the ice cream business. He permits the manufacturer to change layouts, alter displays, change items, and run promotions. The manufacturer is closely involved in the retailer's internal activities, including pricing policies. In effect the manufacturer is free to improve his merchandising and sales position within the stores to help insure that he will continue to supply them. Industry sales practice is such that the retailer, recognizing the need to maintain high turnover and product freshness, develops a close working relationship with his ice cream supplier.

Both manufacturers seek entry to a client company through the buyer and the merchandise manager. But the decisions about ice cream purchases usually move on up in the chain or group for finalizing. Buyer–seller relations are retained at many levels for the ice cream manufacturers, but usually not for the grocery manufacturers. Whether grocery manufacturers can find a means to alter their inter-company relations to fit the Hendrie's pattern more closely remains to be seen.

HENDRIE'S INC.

Robert G. White, president, says, "Hendrie's endeavors to be a thoroughly marketing-oriented firm and takes a broad definition of itself that goes beyond the basic consumer cognition of it. I would define Hendrie's as a manufacturer and marketer, to varying degrees, of primarily low-temperature, convenience, prepared, ready-to-serve foods."

In keeping with Hendrie's policy of "providing one-stop, inte-grated, low-temperature, specialized products and services," the com-pany interrelated its functional divisions into a unique program of marketing: ice cream manufacturing and distribution; public cold

EXHIBIT 1. *Overall Organization Design, Hendrie's Inc.*

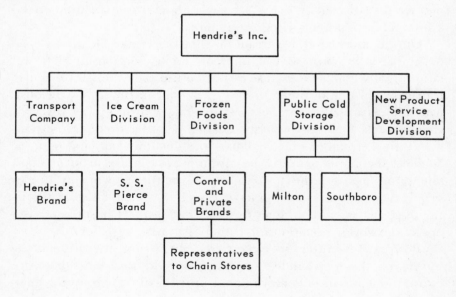

storage warehousing and distribution; frozen foods warehousing and distribution; and new product-service development: marketing and distribution. See Exhibit 1.

SALES SEQUENCE

At Hendrie's managing the sale is a combined effort, just as it is at most companies. The basic steps, or sequence, involved in managing the sale in both regular and major accounts are—

Regular Account	*Major or Key Account*
Area salesman contacts prospect.	Sales representative and/or broker contacts prospect's ice cream buyer.
If prospect might become an exclusive outlet, salesman will bring his supervisor/branch manager into the discussions.	Salesman brings a divisional sales manager or ice cream products manager into the discussion. A Hendrie's senior executive coordinates the effort and acts as resource staff to ice cream products manager or sales manager.
Then, as required, the equipment, layout, and sales plan are brought in.	As required, specialized help is obtained from both in and out of Hendrie's. Executives in other functional areas at Hendrie's serve as staff assistants in the effort.
Once the account is established, the salesman confers frequently with the route delivery man and the customer.	Once the large account is established, regular contact is maintained with such customer personnel as buyer; merchandise manager; grocery sales manager; operations, warehousing, or district manager.

SALES GOAL

Like other ice cream manufacturers, Hendrie's seeks to establish itself within a given retailer as the sole supplier of ice cream products. Unlike other manufacturers, however, Hendrie's has been able to establish such a unique relationship with dealers. Its goal with its dealers is not only exclusivity but also department profit management.

For Hendrie's, establishing this relationship is a major sale. A description of the concept of department profit management is vital to understanding Hendrie's whole system of managing the major sale. Donald White, vice-president, explains the concept: "In department profit management Hendrie's designs the layout of the frozen dessert and/or frozen food cabinet according to sales and profit objectives, traffic flow, cabinet size, investment, and type of trade. Hendrie's prices the products, tabulates movement, summarizes activity, and presents the account with a monthly gross profit-and-sales analysis—by items, by categories of items, and by totals, with computer printouts."

SALES FORCE AND TOP EXECUTIVES

Although Hendrie's is highly integrated functionally, each functional area has its own sales force. (See Exhibit 2.) The top executives, including the functional executives, are all keenly aware of their responsibilities to the marketing activities of the company. All the executives participate without delay or hesitation in helping to obtain, maintain, enhance, or retain accounts—especially major accounts.

Of particular interest in the Hendrie's case is the method and process of its self-appraisal and redirection. As a result of that study, the company set off on a new path that includes its plan for managing the major sale.

DEVELOPMENT OF A MARKETING PLAN

Hendrie's reassessed itself in 1963 and established a long-range plan and a series of short-term objectives. Management engaged in searching self-analysis and developed answers to two major questions: (1) What was the future of the ice cream and frozen food industries? (2) How would Hendrie's fit into the industry in years to come and maximize retailer sales and profits in accordance with its own requirements for return on investment?

EXHIBIT 2. *Functional Organization, Hendrie's Marketing Department*

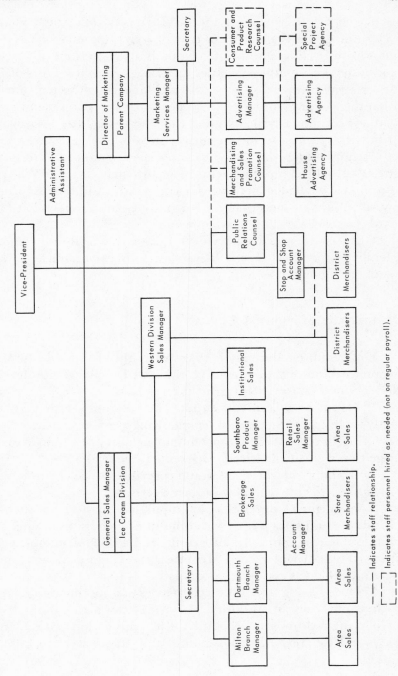

– – – – Indicates staff relationship.

⌐ ¬ Indicates staff personnel hired as needed (not on regular payroll).

So far as the future of the industry was concerned, Hendrie's determined that the ice cream type of frozen desserts would reach a plateau or decline within a few years but that certain product categories such as ice milk, novelties, specialties, and new types of frozen desserts would move on up in sales. Management determined, too, what the ice cream industry well knew: that ice cream manufacturers had few consumer franchises and that there was little knowledge on packaging specifically for supermarket resale.

Hendrie's knew it had to develop a specialty and skill to establish strong initial relationships with new customers. Donald White said, "We knew we had something our competitors did not have: mobility, flexibility, conceptual skill, creativity and innovation, and a hard core of closely knit Spartan people."

Once having resolved its own future role within its industry, Hendrie's was then able to develop an objective and a marketing plan to meet that objective.

Multistage Marketing Plan

For Hendrie's the major objective is the major sale: profitable retailer cabinet management. To this end Donald White developed and set into effect a multistage marketing plan.

1. Hendrie's would concentrate on the younger market, essentially those 18 to 38 years old (emphasizing the young marrieds), representing 70 percent of total potential. Such concentration at an early stage would also avoid stirring up competitive retaliation.

2. Initially, the company would specialize in ice cream novelties, specialties, ice milk, and new frozen desserts.

3. It sought to develop a repeat-purchase pattern through merchandising and sales promotion techniques such as premiums, single and double couponing, trading cards, and a flow of interesting new items. This activity helped Hendrie's enter and remain in outlets heretofore held as exclusive by competitors.

4. Once having developed repeat sales of a specified product line, such as novelties, in an outlet, Hendrie's moved to enlarge its sales by offering a drop-price schedule for a combination order of frozen foods and ice cream. Donald White said, "If we were to fulfill our

marketing plan, we had to have a better product and a creative image to obtain consumer acceptance and competitive prices to obtain retailer acceptance. In addition, we had to be efficient, attractive, and supportive to warrant their continued patronage. But such a policy was too costly to permit profitability. Thus the drop-price schedule was for us a real opportunity to accomplish all we had to accomplish in the market and still do it profitably at a price the retailer liked."

5. This stage in Hendrie's marketing plan is both unique and crucial: *cabinet management.* Once the dealer is willing to permit this Hendrie's service, the probability of his moving to another supplier is greatly reduced.

To bring the marketing plan to successful fruition, Hendrie's applies specific tools: corporate, customer relations, and special tools.

Corporate tools include (1) the corporate overall marketing strategy, which is a combination of well-studied diagnosis and definition of the company, competition, industry, and market, and its evolved long-range plan for growth of market position; (2) corporate emphasis on marketing, creative cabinet profit management, and existing and new product development; (3) corporate flexibility resulting from its four highly interrelated functional areas—ice cream manufacturing and distribution, public cold storage warehousing and distribution, frozen foods warehousing and distribution, and new product-service development marketing and distribution.

Consequently, the close relationship of all these functional areas brings reduced warehousing and distribution costs, increased specialized services, and order flexibility through combined purchases. Hendrie's can therefore compete successfully with larger producers and offer lower prices to dealers without sacrificing quality, service, or profits.

Customer relations tools include (1) Hendrie's seminars. The retailer is brought into headquarters to discuss with Hendrie's marketing people a study that has been done of his stores. The study and seminar will demonstrate to the retailer the profitability of his ice cream, frozen food, and dairy departments (representing up to 18 percent of total store sales); which categories or items in those departments are profitable or unprofitable on the basis of their expense and shelf-space allocations; where and how to display each item for maximum profitability. (2) Computers are used to maintain a steady flow of analyses for each customer. (3) Hendrie's commits 90 percent of its marketing effort to moving its products out of the retailers' cabinets, 10 percent of its marketing effort to getting its products into the retailers' cabinets. (4) Hendrie's assigns a corporate executive to each major customer so that the sales and operating personnel can be fully backed up as needed.

Special tools. Hendrie's believes there are several special factors or tools essential to the success of its program in cabinet management. Donald White says: "First, we must be able to product-manage an ice cream or frozen food department successfully. From Hendrie's side of the program, we must maintain our product and merchandising know-how; we must create a constant mystique in the department that will keep shoppers coming back week after week—and we have to justify our existence in a store by producing high total revenues and gross profits for the retailer. Second, we must be able to design programs especially for each store. A retailer program cannot be plucked off the shelf; it must be designed specifically for the store. Therefore the retailer must be frank with us about his operations; he must have confidence in our suggestions and give us considerable freedom to make changes in layout, products, and prices."

SURVIVAL IN THE SEVENTIES

Donald White is looking ahead and like other marketing executives is primarily concerned with the ultimate goal: survival. He says, "The profit rewards from merely rerunning historical concepts and methods are trivial. In fact, for survival in the seventies, it will be insufficient to merely keep current operating costs trimmed.

"The company that will survive is one that moves to meet the changes in his customers and market. The firm must find its proper role; this is even more important than efficient and economical operation.

"Basic to continuing profitable growth is to take greater advantage of existing channels and networks. We are seeking to get our present customers to buy and use more Hendrie's products. Therefore we must broaden our product offerings and suggest alternative ways to use them. Part of this program has involved tying Hendrie's products in with well-known national brands such as Ocean Spray, Dole, Sunkist, and Hawaiian Punch."

Hendrie's seeks to be totally customer-oriented. Mr. White continued, "Sound, profitable frozen food department management dictates that retailers' total department result is profitable. It is not enough for us to obtain more facings in the 'battle of the shelf.' The sales must be profitable for the customer and for us. As long as we are both doing well together, we won't lose our retailers."

PRODUCT AND PACKAGE DEVELOPMENT

The development of new product offerings in the market is a difficult and time-consuming task that involves key personnel from all functional areas of the company. The development of the package for the proposed new product is thoroughly scrutinized not only by the marketing department but also by production, graphics, the licensor, and by Donald White (see Exhibit 3).

Since new products are added because of their profit potential, cost and profit data are developed through the new product approval form (Exhibit 4). The information obtained is a valuable aid to marketing decisions.

Once the new product is determined feasible for production, acceptable to the market, and potentially profitable to the retailers and to Hendrie's, two checklists are developed (Exhibits 5 and 6). Exhibit 5 shows the ten-phase sequence of company events; Exhibit 6 serves as a list of marketing matters to be accomplished and coordinated before target distribution date.

CATELLI–FIVE ROSES

John F. Ronald, president of Catelli–Five Roses, returned to Canada after 11 years in Mexico and the United States with Procter & Gamble and Quaker Oats. He finds that selling in Canada differs somewhat from selling in the United States: "The concentration of retail grocery sales in the hands of chains and groups is high in Canada, just as in the United States. However, the number of Canadian
(*text continues on page 34*)

EXHIBIT 3. *Request for Product Package Development, Hendrie's Inc.*

Product involved _____ Category _____
New design _____ Modified design _____ Quantity/Yr. _____
Request initiated by _____ Date _____
No. pcs./pkg. _____ Wt./Pc. _____ No. pkg./ship.unit _____Type_____
Type of Container   Paper _____   Plastic _____   Round _____ Square _____
Type of lid or wrap _____
Dimensions of package _____
Type of closure _____
Stock specifications _____
_____

Blank cartons to be submitted for testing _____Quantity _____
Target date for distribution _____
Comments_____
_____

Estimated std. cost/pkg. $_____
Estimated preparation cost/pkg. $ _____
Estimated associated costs $ _____ What type _____
═══

Carton supplier_____ Art by _____
Fanciful product name _____
Product description (legal)_____
Artificial flavor or color? _____
Contents clause: Total _____Ind. serving _____
Manufacturer/distributor clause to read: _____
Ingredients clause to read: _____
_____
_____

Trademarks _____ VH seal _____
All Star license _____ Other licenses _____
Horizontal/vertical face panels _____
Side panel treatment _____
_____

End flap treatment _____

Comments regarding personality and marketing appeals desired _____
_____

Number color proofs desired _____ Number carton sections for POS _____
Is transparency needed for POS or advertising? _____

Comprehensive art received _____ Approved by _____ Revisions _____
Revision received _____ Date _____ Approved by _____
Black and white of final art received _____ Approved by _____
                                              Approved by _____
Color proof received _____ Approved by Production _____
                                  Approved by Graphics_____
                                  Approved by Marketing_____
                                  Approved by Licensor _____
Schedule Delivery Date   Approved by DWW _____

_____

EXHIBIT 4. *New Product Approval Form, Hendrie's Inc.*

Product and name _____

Specifications _____

Pkg./ship.unit/type _____ Size/Weight _____

Branch availability _____ Distribution by _____ Period _____

Justification _____

_____

Profit/ROI Projection	Distribution — Comparative Analysis			
Est. volume ( ) Mos.				
Selling Price				
Est. $ Sales ( ) Mos.				
Cost of Sales				
Gross profit $/%	$ %	$ %	$ %	$ %
Delivery cost $/%	$ %	$ %	$ %	$ %
Selling cost $/%	$ %	$ %	$ %	$ %
Marketing cost $/%	$ %	$ %	$ %	$ %
Admin. cost $/%	$ %	$ %	$ %	$ %
Net profit $ ROI %	$ %	$ %	$ %	$ %

Approvals: Production _____ Date _____

Comptroller _____ Date _____

Marketing Services _____ Date _____

Vice-President, Marketing _____ Date _____

President _____ Date _____

Exhibit 5. *New Product/Packaging Checklist, Hendrie's Inc.*

Name of product _____ Pkg./Shipping Unit _____

Requested introduction _____

Requested by _____ Date _____ Approved by _____ Date _____

		Responsibility of	To be completed	Work started	Work completed	Final approval
Phase 1	**Product/Package Concept**					
Phase 2	**Preliminary Investigation**					
	Production feasibility					
	Package requirements					
	Product costs					
	Legal considerations					
	Market potential					
	Preliminary approval					
Phase 3	**Projections**					
	Distribution					
	Sales					
	Profit and ROI					
Phase 4	**Product Coordination**					
	Package refinement					
	Production sample					
	Product cost					
	Sales plan					
	Marketing plan					
Phase 5	**Product Testing**					
Phase 6	**Product Reevaluation/Decision (Go-No Go)**					
Phase 7	**Marketing Budget — Approved**					
Phase 8	**Advertising**					
	Trade					
	Consumer					
	Merchandising POS					
	Premiums					
	Sales promotion schedule					
Phase 9	**Short/Long-Range Life of Product**					
	6 months					
	1 year					
	2 years					
Phase 10	**Reevaluation/Recommendation**					

EXHIBIT 6. *Approved New Product/Packaging Checklist, Hendrie's Inc.*

Product ____________________ Pkg./ship. unit __________

Project approved ____________ Distribution by __________

Forecast period (___ to ___ , 197_ _____ Month period)

	Responsibility of	Work started	Work completed	To be completed by	Final approval
Sales estimate pipeline distribution __________					
Sales estimate initial sales promotion __________					
Sales estimate 1st ____ wks. __________					
Production requirement – initial 30 days __________					
Sales forecast (3,6,12, ___ mo. plan) __________					
Prod. cost $ ___ August income $ ___ G.P. $ __________					
Marketing plan expense $ __________					
_____ ¢ per dozen/gallon expense					
Coop. advert./sales prom. credit $ __________					
Marketing budget $ __________					
_____ ¢ per dozen/gallon budgeted					
Product Coordination					
Formulas approved and product lab test run					
Packaging design and plates costed and approved					
Packaging cost and delivery					
Ingredient cost and delivery					
First production run – samples available					
Marketing Plan (identify 3, 6, 12, mo. plan)					
Market plan, objectives, strategy, timetable written					
Sales promotion schedule – costed					
Premiums – type, amount, costed					
Couponing and demonst. – type, amount, costed					
Basic POS – type, size, amount, costed					
Presentation brochure – type, amount, costed					
Fact sheets – type, amount, costed					
Trade release date					
Consumer release date					
Food editor/receipe release date					
Advertising production costed					
Trade advertising – type, amount, costed					
Consumer advertising – type, amount, costed					
Direct mail advertising – type, amount, costed					
Trade gift samples – type, amount, costed					
Meeting expense – type, amount, costed					
Trade exhibits – type, amount, costed					
Projects (photo, etc.) – type, amount, costed					
Sales incentives – type, amount, costed					
Professional fees – type, amount, costed					
Communications					
Executive committee coordination					
Procurement coordination					
Production and engineering coordination					
Financial coordination					
Price lists and accounting coordination					
Warehouse and distribution, coordinated and scheduled					
Sales management coordination					
Brokerage and meetings coordination and scheduled					
Distributor sales coordination					
Key account coordination					
Area sales and meetings coordinated and scheduled					
Route sales and meetings coordinated and scheduled					
Special training requirements scheduled					
Switchboard coordination					
Employee and bulletin board coordination					

organizations is far less, which makes it essential that we are well represented in all of them—and that's hard work."

SALES SEQUENCE

The steps in managing a major sale at Catelli can be described briefly as identifying a sales problem; determining who in Catelli is responsible for its solution (the manager responsible confers with those involved in the solution); developing a plan of action; mobilizing for implementation of the plan; making the sales presentation to the customer involved in the sales problem; asking for an order; following through to obtain satisfactory delivery, distribution, and display.

OPERATIONS

Not only must Catelli–Five Roses make certain it is properly represented and displayed in every chain and group; it must also concern itself with the problem faced by all Canadian manufacturers: Canadian income and tastes demand a wide range of consumer goods. Such diversification of products with a population of but 21 million people brings shorter production runs, which can easily result in inefficiencies in operation, a waste of both capital and labor. An executive at a tobacco products manufacturing plant in Canada pointed out that he was able to keep about 62 percent of his machinery going all the time. He considered this a high figure because of the short production runs created by the proliferation of brands and sizes.

"Faced with a fast-rising cost curve, if one of the major retail chains or groups fails to continue stocking and selling the manufacturer's products, the pressure is heavy upon the sales and marketing people," Mr. Ronald said.

Catelli–Five Roses sells through the conventional channels followed by grocery manufacturers—direct to major chains, and through wholesalers to smaller retailers. For this company a major sale is getting its products listed for compulsory distribution in a group or chain of stores. In a disguised example Mr. Ronald describes how the company got its canned soup listed with a grocery chain. Although Catelli–Five Roses salesmen sell to all its client chains, the organization chart in Exhibit 7 shows only the relationships pertinent to this example.

HABITANT SOUPS AND CHAIN X

In a periodic review it comes to light that Chain X does not sell Habitant soups in British Columbia.

The product manager meets with the sales manager to discuss the matter informally and gain some background information. John Ronald says, "The usual upshot of such preliminary meetings is that the sales department looks for ammunition to help it make the sale. The sales personnel claim that the chain says too little advertising is

EXHIBIT 7. *Sales Organization Chart (Simplified), Catelli–Five Roses*

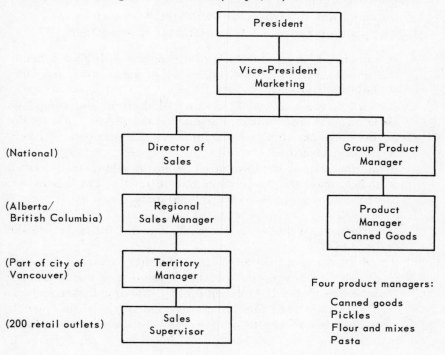

being done. What they want is an incentive to trigger the sale: special price, free goods, an introductory 'cents off' promotion."

THE RESOLUTION

The problem is resolved through Catelli's sales sequence.

1. The problem is identified: no Habitant soup in Chain X in British Columbia. Identification may be made by either the product side or the sales side of the organization.

2. Definition and resolution of the problem is the responsibility of the product manager. He becomes captain of the effort and mobilizes the internal and external aid he needs to make the sale.

3. The product manager confers with his superior, the group product manager, and the whole sales chain down to the territory manager who will be responsible for making the sale.

4. The group (in No. 3) meets to analyze the situation in search of a handle to the problem.

5. A plan of action is synthesized and agreed on.

6. The plan is prepared for presentation to the customer:

A. Product manager assembles from such services as Nielsen a definition of market size, market trend, nature of competition, and share of market and outlook.

B. Product manager assembles research data from the company's kitchens, home economist, and production people and compares the quality and suitability of Habitant soups with competitive labels, private and advertised.

C. A cash incentive in the form of a case-buying allowance is decided on to help make the presentation more attractive. The incentive is offered, of course, to the chain's regional competitors as well.

D. An advertising program is prepared for the market area. Newspaper advertisements including a "cents off" coupon will be run in the entire market area.

E. The district sales manager buys from the chain a packaged promotion program that will permit Habitant soups to be featured in the chain's stores in a special off-shelf display (shopping basket, gondola end) for a prescribed number of days and in the chain's weekly newspaper advertisement, with a prescribed amount of display material.

Mr. Ronald said, "The practice of cooperative merchandising is more intense in Canada because of the limited number of chains and the intense competition for entry into them. The chains must actually limit this activity because of the absolute limitations of space and time, so that the chains are booking promotions about six months in advance. Because of the demand for this activity, chains have raised the price of the promotion programs. It is possible, however, to purchase different levels of activity and restrict the number of stores to recover costs."

7. The whole promotional package is communicated to the chain. At the meeting, which might last an hour, are the canned goods manager, the territory manager, and the regional sales manager. Their audience is the soup buyer and his merchandise manager. The entire presentation will consist of flip charts, a sales discussion, and an analysis of statistical and research data. There probably will not even be a luncheon invitation; but, if there is, the chance of acceptance is slight.

8. Ask for the order. In this case, the request is made that the product line be listed in the chain's computer. This would tell the chain's store managers that the line of soup is available.

The presentation to the chain's buyer and his merchandise manager have been tied to a general promotional effort. If the chain buys the product and the promotion, it has in effect given compulsory distribution of Habitant soups into all its stores in the area.

What is implied then is, if the buyer agrees to list the soup line, the seller gets compulsory distribution, with a specific number of flavors listed; specific initial shipment per flavor per store; permission to set up store displays on a given date.

9. If the chain agrees to stock the soup in its warehouse but turns down the whole promotional package, then distribution is frequently at the individual store manager's option. At this point, the sales supervisor and his superior, the territory manager, contact all the chain's managers in the area and ask them to stock the line.

10. Another option may arise from the presentation. The chain may request a test, limiting distribution to a small number of stores, and review the sales results in 60 days. The territory manager and the sales supervisor must then contact the sample stores and seek advantageous display and cooperation from individual store managers.

3. Installations

THE two major categories of installations are major equipment and real estate. These two costly, long-lasting capital investments are examined in this chapter through comparative analysis and case studies describing how large sales of installations are managed.

CHALLENGES IN INSTALLATION SALES

The sale of an installation, regardless of category, has characteristic problems that differentiate it from a major sale in consumer goods.

Few buyers. The potential buyers frequently are so few and the buyer's needs so specialized that little if any finished inventory is normally carried by the sellers. For the seller this brings a frustrating situation: When he can sell a lot of what he sells, his supply is limited and delivery delayed. This discourages some buyers. The buyer is frustrated by not only the slow delivery but also the fairly wide price fluctuations; when he has no real use for the installation, the price is low; as his desire for the installation rises, it coincides with rising economic expectations and rising prices.

Many levels. Installation-purchase decisions generally involve a number of levels of executives and a broad range of specialists. This is an end result of the cost and complexity of the decision and the potentially serious consequences of a poor decision. Such wide input on the purchase decision creates another dimension of problems for the seller: Sales presentations must be sufficiently well planned and organized to answer the whole spectrum of questions from the buying executives and the specialists. And, since the client's executive levels will participate in the decision, executives of corresponding rank at the selling company must also be involved.

Less personal selling. Although personal selling cannot be disregarded, its importance is considerably less than in consumer goods selling. However, the importance of reliable product information is inestimable.

Delayed decision. Installation sales usually involve a long time span before completion; long-range relationships and patience are integral ingredients in major sales of installations.

Postsale activity. In addition to elaborate presale planning and organizing, installation sales frequently require a great amount of postsale activity. Service after the sale becomes a major consideration in the purchase decision. Thus it becomes necessary in equipment sales that provision for parts, service, and supplies is adequate.

CASE STUDIES

The companies selected for study represent not only two major categories of installation sales but also two very different forms of seller–buyer relationships. The sale of integrated logging systems is traditional in that the seller approaches the buyer; in the sale of industrial sites by Canadian Pacific, the buyer generally approaches the seller.

A logging systems company. This is an agglomerate company engaged in manufacturing pumps, scales, oil field equipment, machine tools, sawmill equipment, and packaging machinery and in distributing pipeline equipment compressors, materials handling and forestry equipment, lightweight buildings, diesel engines, and standby power. It has plants throughout North America, Europe, Africa, and Asia. The sale of integrated logging systems is the area of its total operations selected for study.

Canadian Pacific is the world's most complete transportation system, comprising trains, trucks, ships, planes, and telecommunications. The company is also engaged in hotels, oil, gas, mining, logging, real estate, and paper, both in Canada and elsewhere. Industrial development, the area discussed in this chapter, is one of the functions of the railroad segment of Canadian Pacific.

A computer manufacturer (computers and tabulating machines).

Acme Visible Records, Inc., provides industry, government, hospital, and educational institutions with efficient, economical methods of information storage and retrieval. Acme also serves the computer industry by supplying continuous forms and mark-sensitive checks and by storing and retrieving punched cards, microfilm, and magnetic tape.

Canadian General Electric, which is 92 percent owned by the General Electric Company, has sales of almost $500 million. The company operates 26 plants in Canada, which manufacture products in the following industries: atomic power, chemicals and metallurgical, construction and power distribution, housewares and home entertainment, industrial apparatus, information systems, defense, lamps and tubes, major appliances, power generation, and industrial machinery.

Special Problems in Closing a Sale

In those final moments when the buyer has already received all the proposals from the hopeful suppliers, and has narrowed the choice down to perhaps the two front-runners, two events frequently take place that may shape the whole purchase decision. The buyer may raise the question of reciprocity at the upper echelons of the selling companies, and directors or executives may become involved in pressuring for a decision for their team. The salesman may ask his superior to arrange such high-level contacts with the client company. The director of purchasing in an attempt to justify his existence may step in and demand a price reduction of 2 percent to 10 percent.

These events, while not present in every case, occur with sufficient frequency to warrant mentioning them here. As one sales executive put it, "Their importance cannot be overstated, as they can change the course of the sale." The following incident demonstrates the difficulties that may arise.

A salesman had called regularly on a potential customer for many years but had yet to make his first sale. One day the manager of the client company sought the salesman's advice on a half-million-dollar project. The salesman provided considerable help: He made special trips, helped with the design and layout, and even did some drawings.

The project finally reached the inquiry stage, and the salesman's company entered a proposal. Meanwhile, unbeknown to the salesman, his general sales manager, who was in the area on other business, dropped in to see the vice-president of the client company. When the manager inquired about the progress of his company's proposal, he was told, "Don't worry, your company is going to get the order."

Shortly afterward, the client company's purchasing agent discovered that the whole project had been pending without his knowledge and asked for a 2 percent reduction in price. The general sales manager, remembering his earlier visit to the vice-president of the client company, decided that, since the order was "locked up" anyway, there was no need to give away $10,000. The order was then granted to a lower bidder, and the salesman's company was not considered for the two-million-dollar project that followed. The salesman was reprimanded by the general sales manager for losing the sale, and his upcoming pay increase was withheld.

Major Conclusions

1. *Backup team.* Perhaps the most salient conclusion to be made about the sale of installations is the importance of the auxiliary staff furnishing assistance to the salesman. This backup team, which always includes the salesman's superior, may encompass designers, engineers, researchers, legal experts, technical specialists, and industry specialists. It is not uncommon to include external people such as technical personnel from subcontractors or component manufacturers.

2. *Initial contact with client.* Generally the salesman makes initial contact with a very high-ranking official at the client company—quite often the company president or the division manager—although the salesman may expect to be sent on to the proper person after the initial contact. There is one interesting exception to this con-

clusion: CP Rail waits for the client to contact it for industrial sites. In land dealings this is done for reasons of secrecy.

3. *Preintelligence.* Most of the sellers studied knew in advance what the buyer's general needs were and so were able to focus their efforts from the beginning. Much of the intelligence came from the maintenance selling the companies had engaged in with the client: The sellers had kept in contact at several levels and were generally current on client activities and needs.

4. *Involvement in buyer's decisions.* Some of the companies made an effort to read the buying disposition of the client, and would attempt to improve their chances of obtaining the order through a negotiated sale, high-level contacts, discreet inquiry, or improved prices.

5. *Seller involvement in buyer's operations.* Some of the companies were able to maintain extremely close contact with their customers. Sales and service personnel were at hand at a moment's notice to insure good relations and proper operation of the installations already sold. This served to aid in the sale of future installations by gathering intelligence, developing good contacts, and maintaining the company's reputation as a dependable supplier.

A LOGGING SYSTEMS COMPANY

The process involved in managing the sale of an integrated logging system at this company is divided into three major phases: (1) establishing and maintaining good relations with a number of levels in the client company, (2) learning the client's equipment needs, and (3) negotiating with the client until a purchase decision is reached.

The company's major sale—an integrated logging system—is an integrated combination of field equipment that turns forests into piles of delimbed four-foot logs. With the proper combination of equipment—that is, three feller-skidders and one tree processor—the system will process per hour 150 trees, up to sixteen inches in diameter, into four-foot logs if the snow is not more than four feet deep. Sales are made by the company's own sales force, with strong support from division executives and specialists.

A company executive stated:

If you are going to sell logging equipment, you must go to where the buyer is and talk to him when he is free to talk. Our salesmen can be found in the offices of the major pulp and paper firms, and in the logging camps. You'll even find them sitting late at night in the logging contractor's kitchen after the forests are too dark to cut. In fact a lot of deals are made in the kitchen.

Selling logging systems is quite different in different countries. Language is only one of the differences. In one country farms might be small and not very mechanized. In another country the people might be more mechanically inclined because of large mechanized farms. People in a rugged country may be accustomed to massive equipment to perform massive tasks. Naturally, these different conditions represent different degrees of difficulty in selling our systems. For example, in some places there are still quite a number of loggers using hand-held power saws and horses. And if there is a wedding in the community no logs may be cut or hauled for a week or two. These different conditions have a considerable influence on our costs. For example, in a country where almost 100 percent of the logging is done by small contractors, our sales costs and sales efforts per unit sold are significantly higher.

Obstacles to forestry mechanization. Part of the problem of selling logging systems is a combination of obstacles facing mechanization in forestry itself. Although the need to mechanize is recognized and accepted, the hesitancy to mechanize is still a primary sales obstacle for logging systems.

The pulp companies are pressuring the forestry divisions to mechanize because of the shortage of lumberjacks and the high cost of labor. The mechanical engineers and the forest engineers agree that mechanization is essential, but in many instances they are in a state of indecision because the mechanical engineer keeps seeking fully perfected equipment; and, while the forestry engineer knows all about trees and wood, he is not necessarily current on logging equipment. A great cause of the engineers' ambivalence is the high cost of the system—$200,000 to $500,000. Hesitation to be wrong in decisions of such magnitude is understandable—even though it is not the engineers' own money that is to be invested.

For the independent contractor there may be a general lack of interest in mechanization, often coupled with a lack of financial resources for even the smaller systems available.

Attempts to resolve buyer hesitancy. Two major programs to overcome buyer hesitancy have been instituted in recent years. The first program came in response to customer pressure to lease logging systems. At first this appeared to be a good bridge to resolving the problem, but difficulties quickly emerged. Because of the lack of real commitment that comes with investing one's own funds, the equipment tended to be underutilized, and workers generally were reluctant to accept radical changes in their work lives. The net result was that equipment was sometimes sent back after one year. Effecting work-process change among loggers and lumberjacks, who take greatly deserved pride in their own skills, is a larger task than can be accomplished in one year. It becomes doubly difficult during a short lease period, especially if those affected can create difficulties that will see the lease expire and the machinery hauled away.

The company will certainly lease again but only for longer periods where the lessee will insure effective utilization of the equipment.

The second program, the field demonstration, has already proved successful. The field demonstration is a vital selling tool that permits potential buyers to witness the use of the system. The company contracts with a pulp and paper company to set up a demonstration and prove the value of the system. The pulp company pays for the demonstration on the basis of the logs produced by the demonstration. Loggers in the area are invited to observe; executives of companies that might buy the system are flown in by float plane. The camps chosen are "dry" rather than "wet" camps; no alcoholic drinks are offered. In this instance the company is engaged in what Du Pont calls "pyramid" selling. In pyramid selling key companies in the industry are selected as target markets. The balance of the industry, over time, follows the decisions of the key companies in purchasing such items.

Engineering the sale. As discussed earlier, the whole process of managing a major sale at this company can be divided into three activity phases.

Phase 1: Establishing and maintaining good relationships with client companies. This phase is vital to major sales. Without the close relationships built up over time through sales of parts and equipment and through service aid to client companies, this company would neither be advised of nor considered for major purchases of equipment.

The forestry equipment division purposely maintains close relationships with all levels of its client companies. Company officials feel that they are not in a position to render proper service unless they know what is happening in the offices, the plants, and the forests.

The major clients are the pulp and paper manufacturers. The management of their forests rests with the woodlands manager at corporate headquarters; he is responsible for the tree from seed to mill yard. Reporting to him are the regional or divisional woodlands managers, who are closer to the field activity; the logging camps, reporting to the regional or divisional woodlands managers, are also part of his responsibility. Several executives of the company are in frequent contact at the camp level in the client companies.

The company's field salesman sees the divisional woodlands manager at his regional office. At the logging camps and equipment shop he and the maintenance service representative see additional people who can prove important to the business. They talk with the shop maintenance manager as well as with the maintenance men themselves. They will speak also with the development engineer, the forest engineer, the mechanical engineer, the job foreman, and the machine operators—just about everyone who could possibly bear upon purchase decisions. The salesman will visit with the parts man, help him balance out his stock, help him with his forms, and generally keep him satisfied. He may even spend the night in the logging camp playing cards with the men. In addition the company sends service personnel to visit the logging camp machinery repair shops and also to maintain a close contact with the various camp personnel. This is maintenance selling; all these people may well be inputs to a new-equipment decision.

Phase 2: Learning the client's needs. A considerable amount of information about the client's logging operation is amassed through the company's multilevel contacts. In the field, the company knows the state of each piece of equipment, the nature of the terrain being logged, the parts inventories, and the performance strengths and weaknesses of its own and competitive equipment. Field salesmen frequently are able to anticipate customer needs on replacement equipment and ask for orders as the need arises.

For the purchase of logging systems, however, the recommendation usually comes from the woodlands division level—one step above the logging camp. Systems sales are frequently triggered by the pulp and paper company's marketing department, which is always pressuring for lower prices.

The woodlands division seeks ways to reduce labor costs, and the company attempts to show how money can be saved through its systems. The company makes presentations to the client, demonstrating not only the quality and efficiency of its equipment but financial data as well. Having thoroughly determined the right size and type of system it will recommend to the client, the company presents a configuration of return on investment and discounted future earnings, with production savings considered as income.

Phase 3: Negotiation. Once the pulp and paper company becomes a serious potential buyer, it begins to take a closer look at the kind of deal it wants to negotiate.

1. The forestry managers look over the terrain to be cut to determine which equipment will be most suitable for logging efficiency.
2. The client takes a closer look at its budget and at the company's recommendations.
3. Woodlands division people talk with camp personnel to determine their feelings about various types of machinery and the parts, supplies, maintenance, and problems connected with each.
4. Buyers begin to discuss special modifications, adaptations, and delivery dates; delivery delays of six months are common because of shortages of engines and transmissions, among other things.

Meanwhile, other activity has been triggered at the selling company, also in preparation for negotiating the sale of the logging system.

1. The company's top-level executives are informed, to keep them current and ready if needed.
2. The financial officer begins to lay out alternative payment proposals since most buyers prefer to use their borrowing ability.
3. The supplying manufacturers are notified that they may be called on for special requests in delivery, terms, warranty, or modifications.
4. Suppliers may even send in technical representatives and marketing representatives to resolve any doubts.

Once the purchaser has decided what he wants, when and how he wants it, serious negotiations take place with the company to obtain the system as planned. Interestingly, these orders, frequently totaling half a million dollars, are negotiated successfully without the aid or interference of corporate-level executives on either side of the deal. This is not to say that they do not know what is happening—but they seldom are involved directly in the proceedings.

CP RAIL

The sale of an industrial site—a major sale at CP Rail—is divided into six phases:

1. Contact: The prospect contacts CP Rail industrial development department.
2. Initial search: CP Rail and client jointly search the area desired for sites.
3. Presentation: A written summary of the data gathered goes to the client as the basis for the decision to purchase.
4. Research: Technical and legal research of a narrowed list of sites.
5. High-level inspection: Client representative returns with his superiors to view sites at first hand.
6. Decision.

While not in the business of selling land, the industrial development department of CP Rail must be able to recommend suitable land for industrial sites to manufacturing or marketing companies that ship or receive products and to producers of natural resources and raw materials. The first category of industrial site buyer poses no major obstacles, in that such buyers want to locate near markets and/or labor supply, both of which are near CP Rail. The producer of resources and raw materials, however, frequently poses a difficult decision for the railroad; since nature does not locate its abundance with cities in mind, the railroad must frequently weigh the economic return for laying track into new areas.

Hugh P. McMillan, assistant system manager, industrial development at CP Rail, pointed out that site buyers tend to regard highly the industrial development departments of railroads. (Exhibit 8 shows the organization of CP Rail.) Railroads have no commitments to sites; the major criterion is that a site can be serviced by the railroad. "Our system is large and the possible number of sites very great. We are not confined by the properties actually listed for sale in a given area. In fact, we often show sites that aren't even offered

Exhibit 8. *Organization Chart (Simplified), CP Rail*

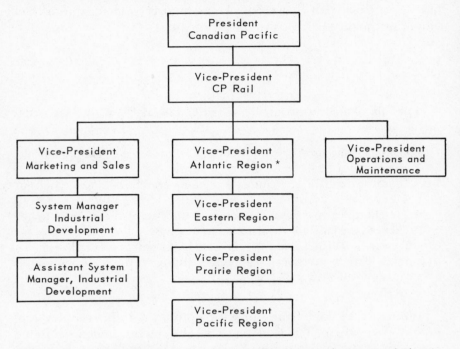

*Each regional vice-president has his own industrial development department, which maintains professional relations with the systems industrial development department in Montreal.

for sale." When asked how he could "sell" sites that are not for sale, Mr. McMillan said, "All land is for sale. It's just that the price has to be right. We are not real estate agents; we are not looking for commissions. What we seek is to obtain shippers for the Canadian Pacific system. For us at CP a major sale is an industrial site that develops considerable tonnage. Our site 'sales' are made through CP offices in very close cooperation with experts internal and external to CP, including real estate firms."

CP Rail Sells a Major Industrial Site

1. *Contact.* At the first stage of CP Rail's sales sequence, the industrial development department is contacted by the buyer who is

looking for a site. The client company is usually represented by an executive such as its real estate manager, vice-president of research and development, or vice-president of production. Mr. McMillan said, "Eighty-one percent of the time the buyer comes to us. All of the major world firms are acquainted with our service through previous assistance in the selection of sites, institutional advertising and promotion, or personal calls from time to time." He added, "It is not uncommon for firms to approach us in great secrecy. We cannot divulge to anyone the firm on whose behalf we are dealing. Some secrecy is so intense that we ourselves are not told the name of the firm, or the real name of the executive with whom we are talking. This places a great burden upon us to decide whether we are dealing with a bona fide buyer. We have had lots of experience and know very quickly whether we are talking with legitimate people. Frequently we are able to piece together sufficient information to know the name of the firms, but then we continue to maintain their anonymity and never divulge even to them that we know who they are."

The giant new automobile plant north of Montreal is an excellent case of corporate secrecy. The executive who approached CP Rail maintained strict secrecy about his company's name and his own name as well. As the executive developed more confidence in CP Rail's industrial development department, he began to open up a bit. This also became necessary as he unfolded his criteria for the site. Nevertheless, not until the manufacturer itself broke the silence after some weeks did the true identity emerge.

For many companies seeking industrial sites, the secrecy is quite necessary so that land sellers do not attach exorbitant prices to their land and competitors will not be aware of their expansion plans.

2. *Initial search.* The client's representative has come to seek a site and with him is a set of criteria to be satisfied. These include size, soil, water, accessibility to rail and auto transportation, accessibility for labor, lay of the land, markets, materials, supplies. The priorities are set out in order of importance, and this frequently presents CP Rail with a problem. Sites in a given area may be lacking in important criteria, and the industrial development personnel may seek to rearrange the client's order of criteria.

When asked about the usual importance of labor supply as a criterion for picking a site, Mr. McMillan said, "Surprisingly, some of the largest and best-known firms set labor as a low-priority item on their list. From past experience they know that their firm is sufficiently attractive to potential employees that employees will move to where the plant is located. The state of the local labor supply is not of prime importance to them."

The railroad constructs a list of possible sites that will serve as many client criteria as possible. CP Rail has a good understanding of approximate values of land in its various operating areas and creates sites perhaps made up of a number of land holdings. The client's representative and CP Rail officials look over the land, possibly from a plane or car, and the list is narrowed to a few choices.

At this point an experienced real estate firm is often brought into the picture for several reasons:

- The real estate firm most well acquainted with values, properties, and people in the area of each potential site is brought in to better establish values and the possibility of completing a purchase.
- CP Rail wants to avoid queering the sale through lack of objectivity; the client may depart if he feels that the railroad is attempting to promote its own properties exclusively.
- CP Rail wants to maintain good relations with the real estate industry.

When values and other factors appear agreeable, the real estate firms then seek to obtain options on the most suitable sites. The name of the client is not usually released, but the sellers are frequently told that the potential sale is to a client of CP Rail and not to land speculators. The whole process of gathering up the necessary options is extremely difficult, as one misstep or statement can destroy the whole deal. Industrial sites frequently are combinations of holdings from many owners, any one of whom can jack up the price for his property, as the following case illustrates.

Sidney S. was hospitalized for an illness of several months after he had bought for $55,000 the building his company had occupied. A few days after Sidney's return to the office, a young lawyer representing the industrial development department of a power company visited him. "We want to buy your building as part of a development going into this part of town," the lawyer said.

"Not interested; I just bought it. Come back in a couple of years," Sidney answered.

Immediately the lawyer said, "You can't do that; you'll spoil the whole development. We've been waiting for you to come back to work. While you were ill we got options on every other parcel in the block; yours is the last one. If you don't sell, it's no deal for anyone."

Sidney replied like a shot, "$125,000; that's it, not a cent less!"

And that's exactly what he was paid.

3. *Presentation.* Once all the data are gathered, they are assembled into an attractive loose-leaf binder for the client's representative to present to his superior—usually a senior vice-president or president. This industrial location survey is a thorough analysis of each site divided into two main sections: the municipality and the land itself.

Municipality information covers such matters as mileage; population centers; population; government development assistance; water sources, quantity, pressure, reservoir, sewers; electricity; fire and police protection; taxes; transportation of all types; and financial position of the community. It also includes a complete list of the existing industries in the area, what they make, and how many persons are employed by each.

Industrial land information includes actual location; square feet in the site, description of the topography, and results of soil tests for bearing capacity; zoning classification; owner; and price, as well as a detailed map and several area photos.

4. *Research.* After options are obtained on the sites, CP Rail then sets its team into action with all possible speed. It is necessary to gather all vital information on each of the sites before the buyer's interest lags. The faster the information is gathered, the greater the time remaining under the option for actual discussion.

The task team is assembled from resources both inside and outside CP Rail. Members include, in addition to real estate experts and lawyers, surveyors, civil engineers, soil experts, water experts, geographers, geologists, economists, rate experts, service specialists, and other researchers.

CP Rail's industrial development people are to draw quickly upon other managers in other areas of CP. They will confer perhaps with their truck, ship, and communications experts, so as to present a more rounded view of the site. Mr. McMillan said, "There is an easy back-and-forth relationship among the people of the various systems comprising the CP. Through such fine cooperation in backing each other up we are able to present knowledgeable, in-depth answers to a client's questions. For example, by talking with our trucking people we can anticipate the questions the client will pose about truck service and rates at each of the sites he is considering. This becomes an important selling tool for us."

5. *High-level inspection.* When the client company's president or senior vice-president has reviewed the presentation—that is, the industrial land survey—he comes to look at the property personally. At this point the client company usually withdraws into secrecy to think the matter over. Sometimes the buyer may try to renegotiate the price of the site and obtain an option at a lower price to take back to his senior.

6. *Decision.* Alone, within its own internal decision-making processes, the client company reaches a decision on the property. If it decides to purchase, the staff of the industrial development department will be phoned and advised.

Mr. McMillan said:

The consummation of a deal is either very fast or very slow; the decision comes usually within two months, or in about five years. The big sales come quite early in the relationship; if the negotiation goes on for too long they break off from pressure or perhaps disenchantment.

We would like to get more involved in their decision-making process, but it would be difficult, expensive and what's more, we could spoil the whole relationship and chase away the client who likes secrecy.

One other thing. When we close a deal for a client, all parties show up—and promptly, too. While our business railway cars are used mostly in developing contacts, land purchases occasionally are "closed" in them. There are handsome old cars with lots of polished mahogany and brass, and an observation platform plus bedrooms, kitchens, and meeting rooms. The car is spotted; that is, situated on the site, and luncheon is served by the steward after the closing of the transaction. It is marvelous; everyone enjoys himself thoroughly. In fact, no one ever turns down an invitation for a meeting on a railway business car.

A COMPUTER MANUFACTURER

The management of the sale at this company is not left to chance but follows a carefully developed procedure designed for maximum effectiveness and minimum expenditure. The steps in completing a successful sale of electronic data processing equipment can be listed generally as follows. At strategy meetings all parties concerned—

1. Develop precontact intelligence on the prospect.
2. Contact the highest-ranking officer in the prospective client organization.
3. Obtain permission and perform a survey of the prospect's operation and define his needs.
4. At the branch office develop a plan of action; get client to attend a demonstration or talk to a satisfied customer in the client's field. At this point probability is determined: go—no go. If probability is low, abandon effort for time being; if probability is high, then finalize the proposal and include an installation plan and a software recommendation.
5. Present proposal; revise if necessary.
6. Obtain order.
7. Implement proposal.
8. Obtain maximum effectiveness.

GOOD COMMUNICATION AS AN OBJECTIVE

Throughout the description of various aspects of sales operations by a company executive in an interview, it became apparent that the common thread was good, close communication.

Horizontal communication. Computer installation sales are very complicated. In addition to the usual sales procedures at the client company—making the right contacts and doing the right things—the salesman is in very close horizontal communication with the support personnel at his office. He is in contact with his superior and with a wide range of specialists in marketing research, technical service, production, distribution, traffic, and marketing communications. While the company supplies the backup people, it is the salesman's responsibility to utilize them.

All through the whole process of managing the sale through to the customer's final decision there is a series of strategy meetings to advise the salesman on each step of the process. He is not alone; rather, he is backed heavily by a support team with which he is in close communication.

Customer communication. Once the sale is made, the company seeks to build long-lasting relationships with its customers. Management knows that, with the emergence of new generations of computers and the virtually constant introduction of new products and devices, present customers, if satisfied, constitute a great market for the future. Thus computer installations are given maximum coverage by the salesmen so that the customer can achieve the most effective results. It is not uncommon for a salesman to have but one to five customers. Some salesmen are stationed full time with their customers and have offices on the customers' premises.

Because of the sophistication of the equipment, its widespread use throughout the organization, and the relatively high cost, most data processing decisions are made at the highest executive levels in the organization. The computer salesman quite possibly may call on the president of a large corporation or organization every day. It is also common for salesmen to develop such close rapport with customers that they are given a free hand to add, or change, the installation as they see fit. This difficult but enviable position is one of ultimate trust. The salesman is, in effect, an in-house consultant on data processing. The client company's chief executive may tell the salesman, "If you think I need the additional equipment [or device], just order it for us."

Vertical communication. Within the computer company there is considerable emphasis on vertical communication—voluntary and involuntary. From the voluntary standpoint, any employee has the right to be heard with impunity at the top levels of the company, if he feels that he has not been dealt with fairly.

Involuntary upward vertical communication is exemplified in the loss review analysis. The loss review analysis determines the percentage of the loss caused by each of four factors and sees how the company stacks up in these areas against the company that got the order. The four areas are—

1. Product: The extent to which product deficiencies caused the order loss. Product deficiency includes physical equipment, price.
2. Programming.
3. Contract and policy.
4. Marketing: Rapport with the account, contact frequency, turnover of company personnel working on the account.

Other factors are also considered, such as reciprocity, arbitrary decision of an executive, consultant recommendation, account's wish to spread the business. Whenever an order is obtained or lost in the data processing division, a critique is held within a very few hours of the event and the next level of management is notified. The company feels that it can learn from its successes and failures. It is particularly important that the loss review analysis be filed within 24 hours so that the next level can perhaps take corrective action—try to save the order and prevent further such losses.

ACME VISIBLE RECORDS, INC.

Acme manufactures and sells record-keeping systems (essentially hardware) in the business equipment industry. Although Acme sells installations, it differs from the other companies discussed in this chapter in that its installations are accessory equipment installations and tend therefore to be smaller sales.

SALES SEQUENCE

The steps in completing a major sale at Acme are—

1. Plan: The salesman's work schedule and sales budget are set.
2. Approach: The customer is called for an appointment.
3. Analysis: The salesman surveys the client's operation to determine his needs.
4. Backup: The salesman utilizes the backup personnel at Acme to create a proposal.
5. Order: The salesman presents proposal and asks for order.
6. Delivery: The equipment is delivered.
7. Installation.

OVERVIEW OF ACME

Leonard Schmitz, chairman of the board and chief executive officer, summed up the functions of the company when he said, "We sell systems. We move paper, not people."

Acme produces systems for expediting the flow of records for virtually any type of information problem. The company produces 11 product lines, several of which are power-operated. The line of products is so broad that Acme can cite any organization of any type as a potential customer. These include, among others, hospitals, banks, the largest brokerage and financial institutions, and the offices of individual doctors and insurance agents. Thus the range of customers is very broad, as is the range of order sizes; the size of an order is not necessarily related to the size of an organization. Orders run from $5 minimum, usually for refill forms, to over $100,000 for a large installation.

SALES ORGANIZATION

J. B. Hinch, vice-president, sales, described the sales organization at Acme: "We have over 400 salesmen operating out of 97 branches. In addition we have more than 500 dealers in the United States and Canada. (See Exhibit 9.)

Acme seeks to hire salesmen who are able to solve problems,

EXHIBIT 9. *Sales and Marketing Organization, Acme Visible Records, Inc.*

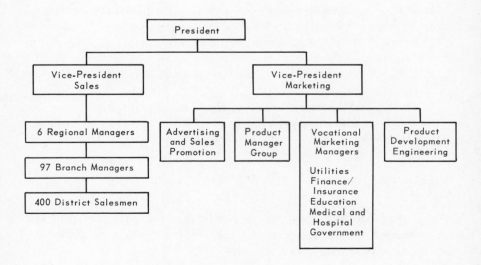

rather than those who are aggressive and will pressure the customers into buying. The cool, logical, analytical, goal-oriented individual has proved to be the most valuable in selling record-keeping equipment. Acme sets fairly rigid moral and physical requirements for those it hires, in an effort to obtain men of good character who will represent the company the way it wants to be seen by its customers.

A suitable candidate is given rigorous training to better enable him to act effectively on his own. He is given a broad latitude for developing and creating systems design, as well as recommending prices and delivery dates. Such authority and latitude are given to the man on a gradual basis as his training progresses, after his superior has ascertained his ability to use this power wisely. Despite the careful screening and rigorous training given trainees, the mortality rate for men in their first year is over 30 percent.

When asked if he was having trouble getting salesmen, Mr. Hinch replied:

Yes, it's a continuing problem, particularly in the office equipment industry, where the bidding for manpower is very high. We find that our salesmen become productive somewhere in the neighborhood of six months. We don't consider a man fully systems-qualified until about two years.

There is considerable difficulty in finding qualified or even qualifiable men. There is generally not a high regard for the sales profession. College graduates especially do not care to enter into selling even though it is a most rewarding career. Eighty percent of the men are quite average; only about 20 percent will go that extra lap or work that extra hour or give that extra bit of help to the customer that will produce the major sale.

We know that a man's supervisor has a lot to do with his performance. It's not always the salesman who is to blame for mediocre sales. The supervisor can make or break a salesman. For example, a very average salesman in Baltimore was noticed by his boss and treated as an individual and blossomed into a real performer. His earnings rose sharply. If a salesman is treated as a person with only average ability, he comes to fulfill his boss's expectation and be average.

Selling at Acme is good hard work that calls for dedicated, sober men who will make all of their calls, complete their surveys, make their proposals, and ask for their orders. There are no shortcuts. If he does his job properly as he should, he will make very good money and be a credit to his family and to his community. And over time, his earnings will increase as the Acme line continues to expand.

Managing the Major Sale at Acme

1. *The plan.* Branch offices plan the salesmen's work on the basis
of a customer record utilizing a visible-card system. Card forms are
supplied covering certain vocational markets such as hospitals, city
and county government, colleges, public schools, federal government,
and companies listed in Dun & Bradstreet at $500,000 and above.
Cards for the various vocational categories are color-coded, and each
vocation card, specially designed for that industry, describes the various applications of the different Acme systems for that industry.

The salesman prepares sales budgets for 30 days in advance; the
budgets are based on the systems that are yet unsold to the companies
in his territory. Sales calls average about 6 per day.

2. *The approach.* The salesman attempts, as much as possible, to
work on the basis of preplanned appointments with the prospective
client. In establishing these appointments the salesman telephones,
specifically stating the reason for the call, "I would like to discuss the
benefits to you of installing a system similar to that being used by
XYZ Corporation."

The philosophy for sales contact at Acme is to start high in the
client company and to have the executive introduce the salesman to
the right person. In companies with up to 500 employees the contact
is the owner or the president; in larger companies it is the appropriate department head. Purchasing agents are generally unfruitful as
initial contacts, as they normally seek only to fill the request orders
and do not initiate orders for new installations and equipment like
Acme's. The Acme salesman, therefore, goes to the purchasing agent
only when he is sent there. If one department has already bought
from the salesman, he seeks to have the department head introduce
him to another department head to pave the way.

3. *The analysis.* Once having obtained an entry into the client
company, the salesman seeks permission to survey its need relative
to the equipment Acme is offering. What Acme is looking for in its
salesmen is summed up in the comment of Chairman Schmitz, "The
knowing how in an Acme sale is to find out the customer's record
problem, and then develop an answer. This is similar to the role of
doctor—who diagnoses and prescribes. The prescription the salesman

comes up with—customer-tailored to the customer's needs—is the nut-meat of the sale."

4. *The backup.* Having completed the survey, or analysis of the client's record problem, the salesman begins to construct a proposal to solve the problem. He utilizes all the help available within his company. The salesman has an open line to everyone at Acme: engineering, production, shipping, finance, and his bosses. In addition, he can call upon the whole marketing department to advise him closely. Acme also maintains a customer service department that will make the actual change-over for the customer from his old system to an Acme system.

5. *The order.* The salesman presents his proposal to the person who gave the authority for the study of the company, and seeks to close the sale with him.

6. *The delivery.* Assuming an agreement to purchase, the customer's order is entered for production, produced and delivered to the buyer.

7. *The installation.* J. B. Hinch, vice-president, sales, says, "The final step in the sale is seeing the item properly installed and operating."

CANADIAN GENERAL ELECTRIC

A subsidiary of General Electric Company, Canadian General Electric Company Limited (CGE) employs 20,000 people in 26 plants in Canada. The company comprises three divisions: Consumer Products, Construction and Industry Supplies, and Apparatus and Heavy Machinery.

SALES SEQUENCE

The Apparatus and Heavy Machinery Division is engaged in the manufacture and sale of turbine generators, nuclear energy products, power transmission systems and apparatus. Harry R. M. Acheson, a veteran sales engineer at CGE and currently manager of order service, described the ten steps in managing a major sale, a drive system for a paper-making machine:

1. Customer inquires about a drive system for proposed machinery installation.
2. CGE engineer studies the inquiry.
3. CGE engineer forwards the inquiry to Systems Sales and Engineering for design.
4. Systems Sales and Engineering prepares a proposal.
5. Proposal is forwarded to the inquirer for comparison.
6. Informal contact period to discern client's reception to CGE proposal.
7. Discussion with client, adjustment, and possible revisions.
8. Final stretch, in which the field is narrowed and the client's purchase decision is imminent.
9. Order is awarded.
10. Postorder activity, including installation and start-up.

Mr. Acheson's area of sales engineering concentration has been in paper machinery for which CGE produces drive systems for the paper-making machines. The drive system is the large and complicated electrical mechanism that powers and delicately synchronizes the Fourdrinier, suction rolls, felt presses, dryers, calendar, and reel of the paper-making machine. These machines manufacture paper at the rate of about 30 miles per hour, starting with a thin soupy mixture that is 99.6 percent liquid. The drive systems sell for about $500,000.

Mr. Acheson is a firm believer in the fundamentals of selling, and has applied them for many years. He is no respecter of the transient salesman: "I believe in making regular calls on my accounts whether they are buying or not. By calling regularly I can keep posted on what's happening in the industry and who is considering new equipment and new plants. I can't really tolerate the opportunistic salesman who only shows up when the word of a potential order gets out. I know in advance when an order is pending."

It became obvious in interviewing Mr. Acheson that one must possess a great breadth of sales and technical knowledge to sell complicated installations like paper-machinery drive systems. The salesman must be able to work knowledgeably with his own engineering production staff, the client's engineering staff, the client's operating personnel and top executives, and the installation team. This talent must be developed over many years of experience.

MANAGING THE SALE

The district sales engineer has played the key role for the seller throughout the whole process, from inquiry through the contact and on to installation and start-up. All activity at his company that pertains to his client goes through his hands. No contacts with the client are made without his knowledge so as to avoid problems of "who said what to whom." Similarly, the purchasing agent at the client company must serve as the key contact for the district sales engineer.

After the order is awarded, it is vital that the district sales engineer maintain client contact with the purchasing agent in all matters, especially those dealing with money. In addition, the customer's engineer should be notified of all technical changes.

A detailed description of CGE's ten-step sales sequence follows.

1. The customer decides to install a paper machine and sends an inquiry to drive-systems manufacturers. The inquiry may come from either the director of purchasing or the buyer's consulting engineer. It contains details of what is to be driven and what the machine is to do, with specifications in varying degrees of detail according to who has drawn them.

2. The CGE senior sales engineer studies the inquiry and notes whether the necessary information is included.

3. The sales engineer forwards the inquiry to Systems Sales and Engineering, where the most effective system will be engineered. Engineers will search their typical systems and design and detail the proper one to suit the customer's needs.

4. Systems Sales and Engineering prepares a detailed proposal containing a list of equipment, detailed by sections; complete diagrams; blueprint layout of the whole room; detailed listings and functions of all the equipment; price; delivery schedule; descriptive materials and literature; promotional materials; capability ratings of each machine; terms and conditions; warranties; exceptions; and comments regarding subcontracting work. The entire proposal may be more than two inches thick. At this point, three or four weeks have elapsed since receipt of the official inquiry.

5. The requested number of proposal copies are mailed as instructed to the director of purchasing or the consulting engineer, who will make a comparative evaluation of all proposals.

6. The delayed-reaction period after the mailing of the proposal is like waiting for the other shoe to drop. Since the buyer may be evaluating and comparing perhaps six major proposals, the first real response may take half a year, unless the matter is pressing. The sales engineer meanwhile is not idle. He makes discreet and unofficial inquiry of a friend at the client company. "Charlie, did you look over the proposal yet? Is everything O.K.?" The engineer tries to promote a full-dress meeting with the client's technical people and CGE's sales engineer, systems engineer, and district sales engineer. He keeps looking for the decision power center to better appraise and perhaps raise the probability of an order.

7. The customer indicates favor for the equipment, given a few changes or adjustments. He may or may not be going through the same process with all the bidders. Buyers then begin visiting other plants to see similar equipment at first hand and perhaps visit the manufacturing plant.

Sellers begin to get eliminated; haggling takes place. The seller meanwhile steps up attempts to influence a favorable decision by pointing out how trouble-free, well suited, and versatile his equipment is.

8. After the buyer has taken a closer look at the competing offers and viewed the equipment in operation in the field, he narrows the field down to two or three. This is a period of considerable tension for the seller and a point at which the buyer may seek some advantage or further price accommodations.

9. The order is awarded.

10. Following the order, a meeting is arranged for the client's engineers and consultants, the machinery manufacturer's personnel, and CGE personnel, including the systems sales engineer, district sales engineer, and systems design engineer. The details are thrashed out and communications arrangements determined so that close contact will continue to completion.

The production of the drive system, which will take six to ten months to complete, will be subject to numerous changes all the way through to installation and start-up.

EXHIBIT 10. *Communication Between CGE and a Client Company, with Backup from Order Service Group*

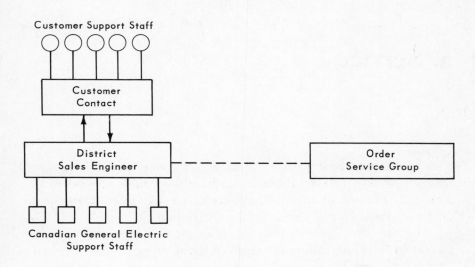

THE ORDER SERVICE GROUP

In the previous section it was noted that the district sales engineer plays the key role in the ten-step process from inquiry to machinery start-up. His counterpart on the customer's side is the purchasing agent. A well-defined intercompany communications channel is a necessity because of the complexity of the relationship and the many months over which the relationship must go smoothly.

At CGE the district sales engineer gets substantial and much-needed help because he usually has a number of installations pending at any one time. The Order Service Group, headed by a senior engineer, serves to back up the district sales engineer after the order is received. The group can service a number of sales at one time and serves as staff support in the process of seeing the order through to start-up and effective operation.

The well-defined and smooth-flowing intercompany relationship is a function of the Order Service Group. The result of such a clearly defined communications channel prevents the chaos of numerous cross-calls and misunderstandings (see Exhibit 10).

4. Services

THE great recent growth of the service segment of our economy adds to the importance of studies on how large sales of services are managed. Because of the wide variety of services offered, six quite different types of service companies were studied.

The size of the service industry is ample evidence of its current success in fulfilling industrial needs. A great proportion of the services are offered by external companies—companies specializing in supplying services to other companies. External service companies offer many advantages to an industrial or business company that permit the buyer to—

- Use his capital for more productive investment than service equipment.
- Charge off service expenditures in the current year.
- In labor-intense services, reduce irritation, labor costs, and labor turnover.
- Predetermine service costs and thus remain within budget.
- Release space for more productive use.
- Benefit from the expertise of specialization.

Buyers, therefore, are not so much faced with the question whether to buy an offered service; instead, they must ask themselves how much of the offered service is suitable for the buyer's needs and from which company the service should be purchased.

The successful completion of major service sales requires that the selling companies give highly satisfactory answers to those two questions. This chapter will describe how they manage this process.

CHALLENGES IN SELLING SERVICES

Services play an essential role in industrial and business operations in that they permit managers to concentrate solely on the business of the company while charging others with the responsibility of service. Despite the desirability of a company's having someone else worry about the service details, the service companies still find eight major challenges both in making sales and in keeping clients sold on the services.

1. Some companies have yet to recognize the need for some services, such as group insurance and in-plant feeding systems.

2. Some companies feel they can furnish services more advantageously themselves.

3. Some companies are reluctant to permit outsiders to operate on their premises.

4. Once the service has been sold, those three problems do not necessarily disappear. The result frequently is that the supplier must continue periodically to resell himself to the client. This is especially true at contract renewal time.

5. The service program must be tailored specially to each client's needs. Too much service will result in waste and possible losses for buyer and seller; too little service will create ill will and loss of customers.

6. The concept of buying a service from an outside supplier is based primarily on the service company's low cost and expertise resulting from its economies of scale of operation and its specialization. It becomes increasingly possible, then, that as the client company grows in size it can provide for itself at a lower cost many of the services it buys.

7. The seller of a service is vulnerable in the event of client dissatisfaction, but he has no one to whom he can pass the blame. The wholesaler can blame the producer; the manufacturer can blame his component manufacturers. But sellers of telephone service, freight service, group life insurance, employee feeding service, and aerial mapping service, for example, must accept all errors as their own.

8. Each service company, and each buyer of services, is quite aware that service companies are easy to replace.

Case Studies

The six service companies studied here represent a spectrum of types, ranging from the highly competitive to a regulated monopoly.

1. Air Survey Corporation, Reston, Virginia, a photogrammetric engineering company that creates engineering maps to very close scale.
2. A telephone company.
3. Canadian Pacific Freight Sales, Montreal, Quebec, a part of the Canadian Pacific total transportation system.
4. The Lincoln National Life Insurance Company, Fort Wayne, Indiana.
5. The Macke Company, Cheverly, Maryland, a vending and food service company.
6. D. H. Overmyer Company, Inc., New York City, a warehousing and distribution company.

Major Conclusions

Supplier vulnerability. The very term "service" implies a continuing relationship, probably renewable at specified intervals, and a commitment to perform a function for the client rather than to merely deliver products. Service requires, therefore, a greater amount of maintenance selling and immediate attention to friction in the relationship than product selling does, if customers are to be retained.

Need for an anchor account. Once a company has agreed to perform a service for a customer, it has an ongoing obligation to continue that performance even if at a loss. Such losses frequently occur as the seller moves into new geographic areas where its market is not yet sufficiently developed. This is a particular point of caution for CP Rail, Macke, and Overmyer, each of which always seeks an anchor account in a new area to at least cover overhead expenses.

The account survey and proposal. It is standard procedure for the telephone company, CP Rail, Lincoln National Life, and Macke to seek to perform a study to learn the prospect's needs. From this a proposal is drawn up and presented to the prospect for approval.

Selling an intangible. In the sale of a service or service contract, the buyer is purchasing an intangible. This is hard for the seller to demonstrate and therefore places a greater seller reliance on sales planning and strategy. (See the section in this chapter on the proposal meeting.)

Negotiated sale. All the service companies studied used some sort of negotiated sales arrangement with their clients whenever possible. Explicitly, Air Survey with government agencies; Macke Company where designated as preferred vendor; and Overmyer with its national warehousing contracts.

VARIATIONS IN THE SALESMAN'S FUNCTION

Among the various companies discussed in this chapter, there appears a discrepancy as to the primary function of the salesman.

At Air Survey, although the salesman does fill an order-getting function, his main effort is in seeing the order properly completed within the company and serving as a liaison with the customer.

At the telephone company both the data salesman and the major account salesman are primarily concerned with account maintenance. The major account salesman is frequently assigned to only one account, where he actually has an office.

At CP Rail the freight salesmen are engaged almost daily in maintaining continuing business relationships with their major accounts.

At Lincoln National Life the salesman is trained primarily in obtaining orders, not necessarily in maintaining accounts.

At Macke the industrial salesman is interested in selling systems —order getting. His secondary responsibility is maintaining relationships with the account, but this appears to be a less appealing activity to men who land large accounts.

At Overmyer the salesman's function is to arrange for a meeting at which teams from both Overmyer and the customer attempt to negotiate a contract.

THE PROPOSAL MEETING

The following discussion is offered separately from the cases from which it is drawn to guarantee the anonymity of the companies that supplied the information. The discussion is a composite and cannot be attributed solely to any one company.

The sale of a service is frequently the sale of an intangible. The buyer is handicapped because he must make decisions based on his perceptions of what the seller has demonstrated to him. The seller is handicapped as he can show little that is palpable. At best he can demonstrate a similar installation that was made at another company.

Many major sales are concluded at the proposal meeting, in which the selling team mounts a major effort for the buying team. The ultimate purpose of the meeting is to produce sufficient information for a decision regarding the seller's proposal. At the meeting sellers therefore seek to make a positive impression on the buyers, create and maintain a favorable atmosphere in the meeting, dispel buyer's doubts, and forestall serious objections or delays relative to the proposal to buy.

The sellers prefer a meeting in which there is an absence of staff who traditionally delay decisions—attorneys and accountants, for example. No proposals are given out in advance so that competitors don't get them and so that those who will attend the meeting will have no time to build serious objections. The sellers seek to present their proposal, answer questions, and obtain a favorable decision at the meeting, but this is not always the way it turns out.

When various members of the buying team voice their objections, the sellers make note of several important facts: the nature and tenor of the objections—whether they are legitimate or obstructionist; who has raised the objection and what are his formal and informal roles in the organization; where the decision-making power lies in the organization.

If it looks as though the meeting will not produce a decision, the sellers seek to set another meeting before adjournment. Prior to the next meeting they attempt again to build a favorable atmosphere by arranging submeetings with those who have raised objections, and with those who appear to hold the power in the group.

AIR SURVEY CORPORATION

Air Survey Corporation, a subsidiary of Lockwood, Kessler & Bartlett, a consulting engineering company, creates engineering maps for government and business organizations. Typical clients include the U.S. Army Corps of Engineers, the Bureau of Public Roads, city governments, public utilities, consulting engineers, and industrial companies.

NEW, REPEAT, AND NEGOTIATED SALES

The sequence of steps in concluding a major sale for Air Survey follows a varied pattern according to the type of client being dealt with. For new accounts the typical sequence would be—

1. Obtain lead of possible mapping contract.
2. Visit the top executive officer of the company.
3. Be referred down by the top executive officer to the right technical people and to those who will use the maps.
4. With the recommendation of those contacted at the prospect company, obtain the order from the purchasing agent.

Repeat sales form the greatest segment of Air Survey's business. Such sales follow a less complicated sales pattern, with a technical rather than a marketing orientation; that is, in repeat sales steps 1 and 2, as well as part of step 3, could be eliminated. Instead, Air Survey's representative would go directly to the customer's technical people and get an order from the purchasing agent. The representative would not have to bother establishing himself, as he would in the case of a new sale.

REPEAT-SALES CONTACT PATTERN

Customer	Contact	Buyer
Utility	Transmission engineer	Contact buys, but final authority may come from a vice-president.
City	City engineer or city planner and director of public-works	Contact buys; sometimes city council O.K.'s.
Private Consulting Engineers	Small: owner or partner Large: chief civil engineer	

REPEAT-SALES CONTACT PATTERN

Customer	*Contact*	*Buyer*
U.S.A. Corps of Engineers	Small district: chief engineer Large district: chief of surveys	Contact buys.
Bureau of Public Roads	District photogrammetry expert plus his supervisors	Regional director buys.
Industrial Companies	Varies as to company and needs	Sale always ends with purchasing agent.

The company usually seeks negotiated contracts rather than bid contracts because of the high cost of assembling bids and the reduced probability of obtaining contracts through bidding. Air Survey does not consider itself a source for clients who place price before quality. The following is an example of a negotiated sale at Air Survey.

1. From past experience and from suppliers interested in performing a given project, the buyer selects and ranks prospective companies in order of preference.
2. Buyer opens negotiations with company number one, asking for its price on the project. The buying company has meanwhile estimated the job for itself, so that it can compare its figures against the bid. If number one's bid is within a 10 percent tolerance, the buyer accepts the bid.
3. If number one's bid is outside the 10 percent tolerance, the buyer will review the bid in each of the four phases (aerial photography, field control, stereo compilation, and drafting) and attempt to bring the bidder into line.
4. Failure to arrive at a meaningful agreement with number one will bring the negotiations to a close, and the buyer moves on to bidder number two to resume the whole process.
5. Once a bidder has been closed out of a negotiation, he stays out; he comes back only in another project.

Nature of Operations

John Wallace, president of Air Survey, explained the nature of the company's operation.

Although the average contract is for many thousands of dollars, the number of contracts is relatively small, so that the sales function can be accomplished by two men—including myself. Generally the territory is divided between us, but we work as a team in closing major sales. We depend heavily also upon several key people in the firm: first, the production manager, who estimates the field control surveying; second, the compilation department; and third, the drafting department manager.

If I explain briefly a typical project, you will have a better idea of how our time must be allocated. As you will see, time is absolutely crucial in our business. Our typical project breaks down into four phases: aerial photography; field control (surveying); stereo compilation (in-house plotting of the map); and drafting. Such a project is a major sale for the company. The limiting factor in this whole operation is the aerial photography, which is dependent upon those cloudless days in the spring after the snow has gone and before the foliage has emerged, so that the terrain is clearly visible. The in-house segment of the work can be done any time, but not the photography.

Mr. Wallace continued, "Because the end product, the map, is the number one item on the critical path for highway and power transmission right-of-way, considerable customer pressure builds for map completion. The weather bottleneck built into the operation sometimes causes customer discontent, and we must try to alleviate that. This discontent sometimes brings us new accounts, as our competitors have the same constraints as we do."

SALESMAN'S FUNCTION

The salesman spends the major portion of what could be called selling time in administering the contracts he has already obtained. The salesman serves as the client's liaison with Air Survey; his talks include drawing up a plan of action that defines the final product, the methods and procedures to be used, the schedule for production, and the delivery dates; formulating the contract; overseeing the estimating; following the whole process through to completion. Thus, with the responsibility of administering all the contracts that he sells, the salesman's time allocation becomes extremely crucial.

While it might be argued that the salesman's time should be allocated to selling and that specialists should administer the order, Mr. Wallace points out that the number of potential clients is somewhat limited. In addition, there is no one who knows better what the customer really wants than the man who negotiated the contract.

A Telephone Company

In addition to the traditional telephone services it furnishes, the company rents data communications equipment and circuits, and facilitates communications between man and computer and between computers. The company is thus better described as a communications company than as a telephone company.

Sales Sequence

The steps in concluding a major sale depend on the complexity of the client's needs and what is being sold. Generally, however, major sales would be the most sophisticated and complex installations and would be covered by data salesmen and major account salesmen. A normal sequence for such a sale would develop as follows.

1. A salesman is assigned to an account—quite possibly his only account.

2. Salesman asks account's top executive in communications decisions if he can study the client company's communications needs and develop a program for keeping up with its needs.

3. Once granted permission to perform the study, the salesman then—

- Determines what the customer's vital pulse point is; that is, what information the customer needs most often and most quickly.
- Determines how much in terms of dollars the customer is willing to pay for that information. Assuming that the more expensive installations produce the fastest results, the salesman must determine the value of that information to the client in terms of cost to get it (cost/ effectiveness).
- Calls in his backup personnel.
- Designs a system for the customer.

4. On completion of the study, the salesman will seek customer approval from the top executives of client company, or perhaps even from the board of directors. The idea is to show the customer how it can cut its costs or increase its earnings.

FUNCTIONS AND OPERATIONS OF THE SELLING ORGANIZATION

The selling organization contains four levels of salesmen, as shown in Exhibit 11, each assigned to account lists designed for certain degrees of complexity.

Major account salesmen and data salesmen, as mentioned, are engaged in the major sales—the most sophisticated and complex installations. The major account salesman is responsible for all communication within just one company and even maintains an office on the customer's premises, devoting his full work schedule to that company alone. He analyzes current operations, foresees improvements, and generally insures that telephone company services keep up with the client's growing needs.

The data salesman sells the man–computer and computer–computer business communications systems. He considers interface specifications, transmission rates, code type, transmit–receive capabilities, number of units, auxiliary service needed, compatibility of the cus-

EXHIBIT 11. *Sales Organization, a Telephone Company*

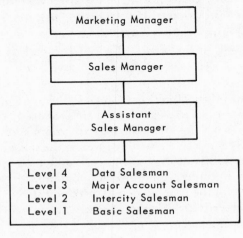

Marketing Manager	
Sales Manager	
Assistant Sales Manager	
Level 4	Data Salesman
Level 3	Major Account Salesman
Level 2	Intercity Salesman
Level 1	Basic Salesman

tomer's computers and photocopy equipment with telephone equipment.

Major account salesmen and data salesmen receive a great amount of support and technical backup in accomplishing their job. A primary source is the salesman's own superior, who can grant approval for many of the special items the salesman feels are necessary to the installation. Advice on selling and implementation, and on sales methods and new products, comes from the methods and products staff; various engineering staff people give advice on rates and tariffs, circuitry, and customer services. The data salesmen have available to them a special intercompany committee composed of one member from each major department of the company plus special experts in critical areas.

To become a fully trained data salesman at the telephone company takes several years, and the company invests upward of $35,000 in special courses and training schools. This intensive training is important because, in making calls on their clients, the salesmen will start with the top executive in communications decisions and, on completion of the study, will seek client approval from the top executives of the company or perhaps even the board of directors. Data and major account salesmen frequently are recruited from the basic and intercity salesmen.

Salesmen sell communications through a carefully determined plan called "Time Programming," operated approximately as follows. Each salesman, each month, is assigned accounts by his superior, and together they determine what the customer's needs are and the number of hours necessary to visit the account and sell him on that installation—in effect, a time log. At the end of the month the sales manager brings in each salesman to—

- Carry out an informal personnel review, during which the manager reviews closed cases in relation to their produced revenue and time required to make the sale and the status report on closed cases. In addition, he completes a coaching form on the salesman.
- Analyze the results of their conference and thereby develop objectives for the upcoming month, new programs, revenue predictions, and estimates of the time needed to meet objectives. Accounts are reviewed to determine which ones need attention.
- Make new assignments.

COMMUNICATIONS SEMINARS AS A SELLING TOOL

In addition to the carefully thought through studies prepared by the company for its major sales efforts, the company utilizes communications seminars, held in Chicago, New York, and Washington.

The company has found that, when its major salesmen were performing a cost/effectiveness study for their accounts, the customer frequently was unaware of his own needs. In effect, the customer seldom knew what information he had to have or wanted; he did not know how fast he needed it or how much he should spend to obtain it. The company therefore suggests to business executives that they attend a one-, two-, or three-day seminar on communications. The seminars are designed to acquaint the executives with the information explosion; with the staff's expertise (and to inform them that such expertise is free); and also with program information techniques. The seminars also cover all kinds of equipment other than the company's.

Seminars are so designed that the first day is principally for executives, and the discussions are essentially nontechnical. The second and third days are designed for the executives' technical people, although the executives are welcome if they choose to stay. The companies pay for the executives' transportation and lodging. A cross section of companies represented at these seminars would include railroads, banks, insurance companies, and department stores.

The final objectives and results are faith in the company's system and added business.

CANADIAN PACIFIC FREIGHT SALES DIVISION

Freight sales, the backbone of the railroad business, are vital to the success of CP Rail, Canadian Pacific's railroad division. CP Rail is a major segment of the Canadian Pacific total transportation and communications system, which includes in addition CP Ships, CP Air, CP Express, CP Transport, CP Hotels, CP Telecommunications, CP Investments, and Smith Transport. CP Rail, where this study has concentrated, provides rail service all across Canada and into some parts of the United States.

Sales Sequence

The sequence of steps in making a major sale at CP Rail are as follows. Exhibit 12 shows the sales organization.

1. The freight salesman, performing his selling duties, reports a major opportunity to the district manager, his immediate superior.

2. If the idea is acceptable, the district manager formulates a marketing plan and sends it on to the regional manager, his immediate superior.

3. If the plan is workable, the regional manager asks his staff assistant, the industrial service representative, to develop a study of the matter.

4. If the industrial service representative's findings are positive, he returns the plan to the regional manager, who takes action if the idea is not interregional; or sends the idea to the system manager–freight sales if the idea is interregional and ready for implementation; or sends the idea to the system manager–marketing planning if the idea is interregional but not fully prepared for implementation.

5. When a plan is sent to the system manager–freight sales and meets with his approval, he will implement it. When a plan is sent to the system manager–marketing planning and meets with his approval, he will have it thoroughly studied and developed by a team of experts.

6. The system manager–marketing planning, working in close cooperation with his experts, with the system manager–freight sales, and with various regional and district men, will develop a workable plan to be implemented.

7. Assuming the plan is to be sold to a specific customer or group, it will be presented to the buyers at a proposal meeting.

Key Sales Variables

C. C. Watson, system manager for freight sales, pointed out, "There are three key variables involved in selling freight transportation. (1) *Service:* While the major track routes are relatively inflexible, they can be and are modified to meet specific circumstances, but scheduling is quite flexible; (2) *equipment,* which is flexible in that

EXHIBIT 12. *Sales Organization, CP Rail Freight Sales Division*

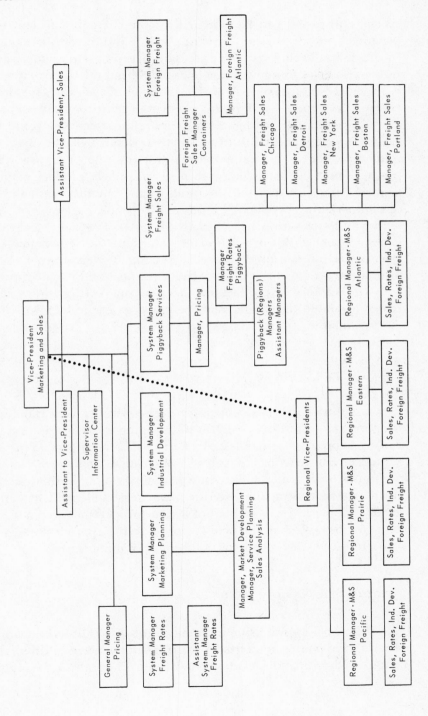

special equipment can be designed for the client if sufficient use is promised; and (3) *pricing*, which is flexible in Canada since the rate structure has been freed up. Rates and pricing are now more realistically related to freight volume in Canada than in United States."

The whole process of obtaining large-volume shippers for the rail system necessitates not only the use of those three variables but also a well-coordinated selling team keeping close market contacts at all levels. In essence, CP Rail uses two opportunities: the direct sales contact by the sales representatives and the sale of transportation packages or systems that have been developed by product managers or marketing directors and then sold by the salesmen with the help of the marketing people. All levels of CP people are engaged in the selling function—from top officials on down. Frequency of contact increases farther down the line. In addition, the system manager— freight sales takes a predetermined number of companies each year (usually five to eight) as "national accounts" and, in conjunction with the applicable product managers or marketing directors, develops a salable marketing plan designed to expand CP's share of those companies' transportation market.

INFORMATION FLOW

Communication and cooperation are especially important in an organization as far-flung as CP Rail. Keeping ideas and information flowing represents a major part of the CP sales effort; as the sales sequence indicates, the company has a clear-cut channel for upward communication. But at CP information flows in both directions. Headquarters conceives marketing plans quite independently of the regions. When it devises a plan of action for a certain commodity or for a specific customer, the plan is sent on to the appropriate regional marketing and sales people for polishing and implementation.

FUNCTIONS OF VARIOUS SALES PERSONNEL

CP Rail believes in using frequent direct sales calls to keep abreast of what's happening in the field. Freight salesmen are in direct daily contact with U.S. and Canadian companies. They talk at the regional level with the manufacturers' traffic managers, distribution managers, export managers, import managers, and coordinators. (See Exhibit 13.) They then report opportunities.

The regional and district freight sales managers call on the same people as the freight salesmen do. They seldom call any higher in the client company. Their time is spent in supervising and selling with freight salesmen, using among other things luncheon and dinner contacts.

The system manager–freight sales and the vice-president–marketing and sales, in addition to their supervisory and support roles for their subordinates, call on buyers at the vice-presidential and presidential levels. In fact at CP any of the top executives may be called in for his help, in that it often takes a man of equal rank to the buyer to close the sale. Mr. Watson said, "In my own experience, upper-level executives in the client firms will speak more freely with me than with my salesmen."

He continued, "Let me tell you about the industrial service representatives in our freight sales. They advise our regional managers–freight sales. These men typically have university degrees; however, promising young men without a university background also

Exhibit 13. *Sales Contacts, CP Rail*

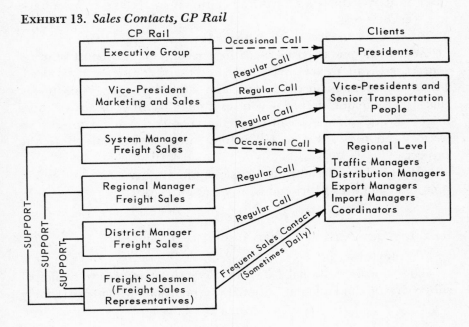

have an opportunity for this position. They fill a unique, creative role in that they conceive new sales ideas, solve problems, serve as a resource to the salesmen, and explore and develop ideas that come up through the sales organization to them.

"We utilize other support personnel as well as the industrial service representatives. The whole sales effort may include experts in pricing, marketing planning and development, scheduling, car design, and mode of power. Anyone in the company that can turn the trick."

SPECIAL CONSIDERATIONS FOR NEW FACILITIES AND EQUIPMENT

In formulating a major sales proposal, the railroad must take into consideration several important cost considerations.

First, some sales involve continuing service, which means a large outlay in equipment, sidings, special design, and training of personnel. For example, the railroads have invested heavily in special cars and terminals for auto carriers, piggyback freight, and containerization—three major innovations in recent years. With innovations, there is always the question whether they will receive sufficient use to cover their cost.

Second, CP is faced with a somewhat similar problem in the development of new deposits of natural resources. Frequently the resource find is in an area not serviced by the railroad; or, if serviced, the facilities are inadequate for major shipments. Mr. Watson says that, when the question of new or expanded facilities arises, CP does a serious study of the potential of the area, the demand for the resource, and the return to CP before funds are committed to the project.

Finally, the railroad must consider the alternate and additional uses for any new facilities and equipment purchased.

THE LINCOLN NATIONAL LIFE INSURANCE COMPANY

The Lincoln National Life Insurance Company is the principal subsidiary of the Lincoln National Corporation, which is a widely diversified financial services organization marketing almost all forms of individual and group life and health insurance, as well as fire and casualty insurance. Through Lincoln National's Equity Sales Corporation, variable annuities and mutual funds are also offered.

Sales Sequence

In the sale of group insurance, the subject of this case study, the steps in making the sale can be described generally as follows.

1. Lincoln National salesman contacts chief executive officer at the client company and seeks permission to survey the company's insurance needs and current program.
2. Having gained such permission, the salesman gathers the census material, confers with backup experts at Lincoln National, and draws up a proposal.
3. The salesman holds a proposal meeting with the executives of the client company, with the objective of obtaining a master contract.
4. Having obtained the master contract, he sets about enrolling the employees.

Nature of the Business

As American business companies have come to realize in recent decades, their major assets are the human assets—their employees. Part of the entire process of obtaining and retaining good people is the employee benefit program; group insurance contracts have become a major segment of such programs.

Most companies that can use a group benefit plan for their employees have already bought such insurance or at the least have been canvassed often enough by aspiring salesmen to have a good knowledge of the subject. There are no neophyte executives left to be tapped. The market therefore calls for rather sophisticated selling techniques to take an account from a competitor or to sell to the hard-core negativists.

Such a challenge requires carefully developed sales strategies, well-trained salesmen, considerable expert advice to back up the salesmen, and close and knowledgeable supervision.

EXHIBIT 14. *Sales Organization, Lincoln National Life, Eastern Division*

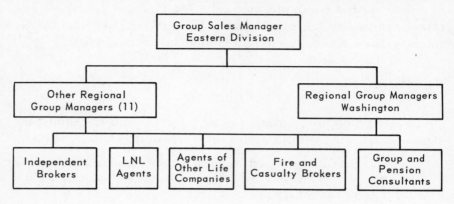

C. T. Hellmuth, Eastern Division group sales manager, described the organizational relationships in his division (see Exhibit 14). He pointed out that the main sales effort for group insurance is through Lincoln National agents; these agents are independent contractors for whom Lincoln National provides certain subsidies and whose contract requires that they first offer any business to the company. The training, the guidance, the backup provided by the regional group managers is aimed primarily at these men, but not to the exclusion of the independent brokers and agents of other insurers. The regional group manager is a direct employee of Lincoln National working under Mr. Hellmuth's supervision. His primary function is the production and conservation of quality group business. His role with Lincoln National agents, independent brokers, and agents of other insurers is supportive rather than managerial. He is compensated by salary and by an override directly related to production and conservation of quality business. Exhibit 15, following this case, is a job description for a Lincoln National regional group manager.

Mr. Hellmuth pointed out the major obstacle to success for his regional manager: failure to make the salesmen independent. The regional manager's earning power is largely determined by the ability of his men to act alone. The more involved the regional manager becomes in the individual efforts and actions of his men, the fewer men he can manage, and his income from their efforts is thus limited.

Success as a regional group manager, according to Mr. Hellmuth, comes from (1) training agents and brokers so that they no longer call upon the regional group manager for minor decisions and answers; (2) weaning agents away to act on their own so that the manager can widen his span of work to more agents and brokers; (3) retaining agent and broker loyalty to manager and company by keeping them up to date on the latest industry information, and by backing up the agent or broker when he really needs it. The net result of such a policy will be to have "more and more competent producers who depend on the regional group manager less and less."

SUPPORT FOR THE SALESMAN

According to his level of training and competence, the agent or broker calls in his group manager at varying stages of progress in the sales sequence of a case.

The aid available to the salesman can come both from his region or division or from the Fort Wayne home office. Regional or divisional assistance generally is sought on techniques or problem solving, or when ingenuity is needed. The assistance available from Fort Wayne is more technical in nature: statistical information; administrative procedures; special contract changes; and overseeing national enrollments. The home office also approves, or reserves the right to reject, proposals made to clients.

The salesman is also given other sales aid, including Lincoln National assistance to the client in developing cost analysis for union negotiations; assistance in the development of new coverage; and booklets for clients to give current and incoming employees.

Despite the great number of specialists, analysts, managers, and hardware available to the agent, it is the agent or broker who must manage the sale through to completion.

THE SALESMAN AND HIS CLIENT

In selling group life insurance to organizations, it is extremely important to start with the chief executive officer (the president), who then will refer the salesman to other people in the organization. The salesman seeks to accomplish two basic objectives in the initial

(text continues on page 87)

Exhibit 15. *Job Description, Regional Sales Manager, Lincoln National Life*

Regional Group Manager

Lincoln National's group department conducts its sales operations through 142 sales agencies plus independent brokers and consulting firms. The annual premium income exceeds 140 million dollars.

The group department's sale of new business and servicing of existing accounts are supervised by 43 regional group managers in 33 group sales offices located in major metropolitan areas. Each office handles a premium income ranging from one million to fourteen million dollars per year.

Responsibilities

The regional group manager is responsible for a specific territory including his metropolitan area and all or parts of one or more states. He works through Lincoln agents, and independent insurance brokers and consultants, in the development and sale of new business, and the conservation of existing business.

With the vital interest by business and industry in employee benefit plans, and the substantial expenditures involved, the regional group manager deals with top management people. These individuals, and the agents and brokers, are often considerably older and have more business experience than the regional group manager. He must be able to work with these people effectively, and to do so in the face of rigorous competition.

The regional group manager must be an effective salesman and also possess technical expertise. He is thoroughly trained to understand and develop complex packages of fringe benefits for employees of any industry. He must be able to contact the leading insurance people in his area and develop new business through them.

He must maintain effective control over, and assume responsibility for, the services and administrative functions. He must be able to work, through direct contact and correspondence, with home office employees at all levels, and coordinate their efforts with the service needs of the client firm and the agent or broker.

Qualifications

1. Integrity
2. Sales personality
   a. Makes good impression quickly.
   b. Exhibits enthusiasm.

EXHIBIT 15 (*continued*)

    c. Exhibits confidence.

    d. Neat appearance.

    e. Expresses ideas clearly—good verbal ability—good conversationalist.

    f. Empathy—ability to put himself in the other man's shoes and find a solution to his problems.

    g. Ego—sufficient ego to ask for the business when it has been earned.

3. Intelligence
   a. Very superior intelligence with emphasis on quick, resourceful thinking.
   b. Can "think on his feet."
   c. Ability to deal intelligently with unexpected developments.
   d. Can turn objections into sales opportunities.

4. Self-motivated—high energy level—strong determination and desire to achieve
   a. Possesses drive—is a self-starter; ego drive.
   b. Can create his own work.
   c. Does not need to depend on direct supervision.
   d. Exhibits aggressiveness.
   e. Wants his income determined largely by his own efforts.
   f. Wants opportunity to run his own office.

5. Stability
   a. Not easily discouraged.
   b. In the face of a declination can move on to the next prospect confident that the prior declination was not due to any deficiency in the product.

6. Versatility and empathy
   a. Is flexible and can adapt himself to varying situations.
   b. Exhibits tolerance and ability to deal with a wide variety of people.
   c. Not a "detail man," but recognizes the necessity for completion of details for success in his operation.

7. Maturity
   a. Is able to work effectively with management people and insurance salesmen who are often considerably older and have greater business experience.

Training

Total training time—14 to 18 months. The first five to six months are in the home office, followed by nine to twelve months of field training. In addition to technical and sales training, emphasis is given to the individual's personal development—particularly his sales personality and management philosophy.

EXHIBIT 15 (*concluded*)

Phase I: Home Office

The program is informal and focuses on the needs of each individual. Training is provided in all areas of the department's operations, including—

Contracts	Specific product knowledge
Rate structures	New business procedures
Administration	Renewal procedures
Claims	Competition

Individual coaching and counseling, and small-group seminars are utilized. Also included are self-study assignments prepared by the American College of Life Underwriters covering a broad spectrum of insurance and business subjects. This program leads to the attainment of the CLU designation (Chartered Life Underwriter), a professional award of real significance in the insurance industry.

Only after technical competence is achieved—an understanding of the company's products and procedures—does the individual begin his field training.

Phase II: Field training—Nine to Twelve Months

Conducted at one of the regional group sales offices under the direct supervision of a senior regional group manager. The individual works closely with the manager in all areas of sales management and field activities, including—

- Initial visits to, and continued contacts with, the leading insurance people in the area.
- Initial interviews and sales presentations to business firms.
- Completion of sale and establishing service and administrative procedures.
- Arranging for continuing service with home office–client administrative people.
- Reviewing and making recommendations for benefit changes and improvements for prospective and existing accounts.
- Renewal and updating plans for existing accounts.
- Conducting sales meetings and individual consultations with agents or brokers.

When the individual has demonstrated competence in the above areas, and in the ability to manage his activities without direct or close supervision, he is appointed as regional group manager in one of the following types of offices:

(A) One-Man Office
  1. Fills vacancy in existing office.
  2. Opens new office in an area not previously handled locally.

(B) Multiple-Man Office
  1. As second or third man to supplement existing sales management staff or fill vacancy in staff.

interview: (1) Obtain, at the president's direction, employee census data and details about existing employee benefit plans, directly from key operating personnel; (2) commit the president to judging his present insurers by current performance—not by what they may do in response to the Lincoln National proposal.

During the initial interview with the president, the salesman asks for the company's insurance objectives, such as cost and benefit limits. He inquires about company limitations on buying insurance and about employee objections to present coverage. In addition he asks for a copy of the labor contract.

After gathering the information, the salesman will review it with the regional group manager, who will aid him in the design of a proposal to be presented to the president. Other executives of the prospect company who are frequently in attendance at the proposal interview include the controller and the labor relations executive.

Mr. Hellmuth described a successful salesman as one who exercises empathy and ego in proper balance. The salesman needs empathy to put himself in the president's shoes and help solve the executive's problems; and, when the salesman has done a good job, he needs sufficient ego both to feel that he has earned the business and to ask for it.

The objective—the major sale—is a master application signed by the president. After that the employees are enrolled in the program.

The two crucial points in the management of the major sale are, first, obtaining the consent of the chief executive to survey the company and, second, the proposal meeting. These are the moments when decisions hang in the balance and a misstatement can obliterate uncounted man–hours of effort.

THE MACKE COMPANY

The Macke Company is a major vending and food service company aimed primarily at the institutional mass-feeding market. It is moving into the service industry more broadly, as evidenced by its acquisition of building maintenance and painting contractor companies. Macke Company currently services business, industrial, governmental, and educational organizations.

Headquartered in Cheverly, Md., the company operates in about 25 states. Food service and vending companies must maintain very close and personal contact in the field, and so considerable decentralization is necessary to give the various geographical regions a very high degree of autonomy. One of Macke's principal regions, the Shenandoah–Piedmont region operating in the industrial Southeast, is the subject of this study.

SALES SEQUENCE

Marcus Kaplan, regional president, defined a major sale for Macke as an agreement with an institution to permit Macke to install a vending system, a cafeteria system, or a combination of the two, a "coin 'n counter" system. A normal sequence for such a sale would be—

1. A Macke industrial salesman contacts the plant manager or director of industrial relations of a prospective account to seek permission to survey the company's food service needs.
2. On receiving permission, he surveys the company to establish the needs.
3. The salesman confers with Macke executives and support personnel to draft a proposal to the prospect.
4. The salesman makes a proposal to the executive or perhaps to a special committee designated for this purpose.
5. If accepted, proposal goes back to Macke for processing.
6. Install and get system running smoothly.

MACKE SALESMEN

The Macke Company's sales force comprises two basic types of salesman: regular salesmen, who call on what is denoted in the industry as "street vending" accounts. "Street" accounts are actually any type of public premises where the public enter off the street and purchase products from vending machines. These include, for example, restaurants, bars, airports, service stations. Developing such accounts is an excellent training ground for the development of the second type of salesman: the industrial salesman. He sells Macke's service system to plants, government installations, hospitals, and schools.

Although Macke serves many of the largest organizations in the country, its major sales are made at the local level. The local plants or offices of national companies usually delegate food service decisions to the local managers, feeling that they are in a better position to decide among the suppliers in the area. Joe Kingrey, vice-president and general manager of the Shenandoah–Piedmont region said, "Our initial contact is with the plant manager, then the director of industrial relations. Before we are through, however, we may have seen the purchasing agent and the board of directors, too. Hospital contacts are with the administrator; school contacts are with the business manager and the school board. In calling regularly on prospective accounts, we seek to contact the chief decision maker, the plant manager in industry, but we always maintain good relations with the personnel manager."

At Macke any of the executives, including the president, can initiate contact with customers to generate sales. Such action would be cleared first to avoid doubling up.

The industrial salesman seeks initially to survey the prospect's operation. He gathers information on the number of people, their sex, and work shifts; he examines the physical layout and available space as well as the hours and pay scale.

THE PROPOSAL

From the information gathered in the survey, Macke can determine the sales potential. This, however, is not the whole picture, and a much closer study is necessary.

With the survey completed, the salesman then meets with one of the executives—Kingrey or Kaplan—to discuss the possibilities. If the prospect shows a potential for profit, then a first draft of a design for the system is prepared and costs projected. If the projection looks unprofitable, the salesman returns to the prospect and asks for a subsidy for the service—not an uncommon way to bring necessary food service to small operations in isolated areas.

For Macke, the question of entering into a new geographical area —one in which it has no customers yet—involves a real moment of decision. Will the newly acquired customer generate sufficient revenue to pay the supplier to establish the necessary local base of operations? If not, are there sufficient potential customers in the area who will bring the supplier's new local base into the profit side of the ledger? And how long will it take to add the needed new customers? The establishment of such anchor accounts is essential to the growing company; yet the cost of having only anchors can be extremely high.

An expanding company like Macke is frequently confronted with this problem. Marcus Kaplan discusses the traditional salesman–accountant dichotomy that arises when accounts are obtained in new geographic areas. "All of us at Macke," Kaplan says, "want the firm to grow. It is sometimes difficult to develop new branches into profitable operations. The salesmen are eager to open new accounts, but the branch manager and his accountants are faced with the geographic spread and the ultimate contribution to branch profit. The accountants don't want the distant accounts because of high costs, and the salesmen accuse them with holding them back. Ultimately the branch manager, Joe Kingrey, or I have to help them resolve the issue."

If after all this discussion the prospect still looks profitable, the presentation begins to take shape. Mr. Kingrey said, "In putting my presentation together I make good use of our resource people locally and in Washington: regional food director, vice-president of food services, dietitian, design engineer, interior decorator, industrial designer, artist, and accountants. The prospects can see what great detail we have gone into and that we know our business—and we know theirs, too."

Mr. Kingrey continued, "I like to make proposals to a group: plant manager, personnel director, purchasing agent, and others. I want to be able to handle all the problems at one time. I bring in multiple copies of the proposal—they are not mailed in advance—and we all sit together and read it aloud. With flip charts I can show drawings, plans, and schematics."

If the proposal is accepted, it goes back to Macke for processing toward installation and operation. When the proposal becomes a firm order, the salesman is no longer in charge of client contact. Now the Macke operations manager takes over and is responsible for the installation process. The salesman stops by, however, to help see it through.

THE NEGOTIATED SALE

Macke avoids bidding for accounts whenever possible for several reasons.

1. Macke considers its services to be unique; it believes that it really does offer a different measure of cooperation with the customer, an added bit of service that is not definable in a bid contract. Marcus Kaplan said, "How can we describe in a bid that our menus are better than standards, and that we are 'crazy-clean' in our installations?

2. "Besides that," Kaplan said, "purely price customers are anybody's customers. There is always someone cheaper, and the 'price' operator will end up with those accounts. The employees will end up with lower-quality products, services, and conditions.

3. "Frequently, too, our bid may not seem quite so advantageous to the buyer, but the difference in quality and service will attract more sales dollars and thus bring the account the highest possible return."

POSTAGREEMENT LETDOWN

The completion of major sales frequently requires many months, or perhaps several years of effort, on the part of the seller. But merely reaching an agreement or contract with the client is for many suppliers only a step along the way. The postagreement period may require obtaining and installing the equipment, performing special functions, and making sure that the service is functioning satisfactorily. For the salesman who enjoys obtaining new clients, the postagreement activity appears anticlimactic, and his interest may begin to lag.

Joe Kingrey cited the problem of the salesman's declining interest in accounts already "locked-up." "Despite our frequent review with the salesman on how his accounts are performing, he just doesn't make his regular calls unless the account is threatened or contract renewal time is rolling around. It's like fishing: Everyone likes to land the big ones; but, when it comes to the cleaning and cooking so that they can taste their success, interest lags."

D. H. Overmyer Company, Inc.

In 1947 Overmyer started out as a warehousing company in an abandoned factory building in Toledo, Ohio. Today the company is a national warehousing–distribution complex operating in 60 U.S. and Canadian cities. It is engaged in public warehousing of all sorts (cold, cool, flow-through, and network); distribution centers on a lease/handle basis; real estate leasing; equipment leasing; custom-built leased warehousing. Overmyer is currently developing facilities for containerization and intermodal distribution to accommodate the new freight problems of the jumbo jets, container ships, and mile-long unit trains.

Sales Sequence

In this study the major sale for D. H. Overmyer is its "One Fell Swoop" program, designed to sell a national warehousing package agreement (a comprehensive warehousing service) to large national companies operating with multiproducts in multimarkets. The ten-step sequence in concluding such a major sale is divided into four main phases.

Phase 1: Setting up the group meeting with the prospect.

1. Prospective customer list is made up.
2. Salesman visits prospect to determine the prospect's needs and establish his eligibility for continued sales effort.
3. Assuming that the prospect can generate sufficient business to make the program mutually profitable, the salesman then seeks to set up a group meeting between decision makers from the two companies.

Phase 2: Preparing for the meeting.

4. Overmyer assembles a special team designed to fit the needs of the prospect concerned.
5. Prospect is told who D. H. Overmyer will send to the meeting.
6. Overmyer team is briefed before meeting with the prospect group.

Phase 3: The meeting.

7. The meeting, composed of decision makers from both Overmyer and the prospect company, convenes with the understanding that possibly the discussions will last for several days. It is also understood by those present that the meeting is not merely a sales presentation, but that they are assembled to negotiate a mutually profitable solution to the prospect's warehousing problems.
8. Assuming a successful group meeting, the agreement is drawn and signed.

Phase 4: Reporting progress; implementing the contract.

9. The Overmyer salesman provides a report of the meeting, whether it is successful or not, so that others may learn from the experience.
10. The contract is implemented.

THE MAJOR SALE

While sales in many of the areas Overmyer is engaged in could rightly be called major sales, this study delves into but one area: Overmyer's program for national warehousing package agreements with large national companies.

The agreement that Overmyer concludes with the buyer—and no two such agreements are alike—is in effect a total distribution plan for the client. Generally the program includes the following points, among others:

- Incorporate the client's own warehousing facilities, even if it is a conglomerate with a wide range of products.
- Set up a national distribution network to handle all facets of warehousing and distribution for the client's materials, components, and finished goods.
- Give the client a preset national rate.

- Guarantee space for emergency warehousing needs.
- Provide an inventory control system with statements and records of each transaction.

One-Fell-Swoop Group and the Negotiated Sale

Robert Schmidt, Overmyer president, said, "There are only about 250 corporations that need the sort of national warehousing package agreement that we are offering. Our company, being a national warehousing company, can work for national companies on a national scale. The big companies have some gigantic, complex, and sometimes unpredictable warehouse needs that may reach into every segment of the country."

William C. Terry, executive vice-president, added, "Overmyer has learned that the difficulties and delays in attempting to conclude a national warehousing package agreement are frequently sufficient to destroy the prospect's interest and our own sales momentum. The result, or course, is a number of lost sales—all of which are frustrating. It is important to us, therefore, that we sit down with the prospect as soon as possible after he recognizes that he has a mutual interest with Overmyer and negotiate the agreement."

Overmyer, therefore, uses a unique approach to managing the major sale. Whereas most companies aim their selling efforts toward closing the major sale, Overmyer's selling efforts are aimed at selling the prospect's decision makers on sitting down and negotiating with it. Overmyer first sells the concept of the national warehousing agreement, then negotiates with the prospect the terms and details of that agreement.

Once Overmyer's sales representatives have completed their study of the prospect, and the prospect has agreed on the validity and feasibility of working out a warehousing agreement with Overmyer, both companies sit down and attempt to reach an agreement. Overmyer is represented at such a meeting by its One-Fell-Swoop Group, which is composed of five experts: (1) a decision maker: a top vice-president who does not have to clear with the home office before closing a deal; (2) an operations man: an expert on warehousing logistics; (3) a product specialist: an expert on distributing the prospect's product; (4) a service coordinator: an expert on the geographic markets in which the prospect sells (after the conclusion of the agreement, the coordinator will remain as service contact with the customer and function as a member of the customer's own staff); (5) a contract specialist: an expert who will work jointly with the prospect's contract specialist in finalizing the contract evolved in the negotiation.

The prospect company is represented at the meeting by its own comparable team of decision makers, each expert in his own area, so that final terms can be reached without checking with superiors.

SELLING THE MEETING

The major prospects for Overmyer's specially designed program are companies that are expanding their product lines and/or acquiring new companies and product lines. Rick Ulrich, an Overmyer sales specialist, said, "Eighty percent of all products in today's marketplace are products which did not exist ten years ago. As manufacturers penetrate their markets more deeply, they invariably add to the number of items in their lines, creating a need for additional warehousing. The current economy is such that manufacturers are cutting back on capital expenditures. The costs of real estate, construction, and money are forcing firms to consider outside warehousing. Our One-Fell-Swoop Group program is designed to provide these prospects with a national price for a guaranteed time period. This is a major point for a manufacturer concerned with spiraling distribution and warehousing costs."

The probability of closing a major sale is quite high once the meeting is held between Overmyer's One-Fell-Swoop Group and the prospect's decision makers. The selling. effort, therefore, must concentrate on bringing qualified and interested prospects to the meetings to negotiate. Care and planning in this effort are essential, and include such special arrangements as—

1. Alphabetized prospect files.
2. Forms for analyzing prospects to determine potential gross revenue per month, so as to determine priorities in selling effort.

3. Appointment information forms to determine where and when meetings will be held; the forms also list the names and titles of each prospect's decision maker, operations man, product specialist, service coordinator, and contract specialist who will be present.
4. A large daily diary to record all vital information on the group meetings.
5. A monthly calendar to keep track of which Overmyer salesmen and executives will be engaged where in sales appointments and group meetings; this prevents embarrassing date and time conflicts.
6. A columnar form for each team to indicate all necessary information and comments.
7. A file of companies that have at present decided against a group meeting.
8. A write-up from the salesman on his success or failure with a given prospect.

In addition to the above Overmyer also utilizes—

1. Advertising aimed at the prospects and concentrating on the One-Fell-Swoop Group concept.
2. Four sales specialists whose primary duty is to concentrate on setting up One-Fell-Swoop Group appointments.
3. Strong effort to obtain from Overmyer's various sales executives around the country an upward flow of information on the approaches best suited to the One-Fell-Swoop Group concept. Such information is then disseminated to the field.
4. Very close support from headquarters for the branch operations.

SALES ORGANIZATION

Exhibit 16 shows the Overmyer sales organization. The chart indicates the persons who are responsible for "bird-dogging" potential prospects for a One-Fell-Swoop meeting, and also shows those who are used from time to time as the decision makers in an actual One-Fell-Swoop conference. As mentioned, both Overmyer and the prospect company are represented by comparable teams of decision makers. Thus President Robert Schmidt participates in a One-Fell-Swoop meeting only when his counterpart is scheduled to be present.

EXHIBIT 16. *Sales Organization, D. H. Overmyer Company, Inc.*

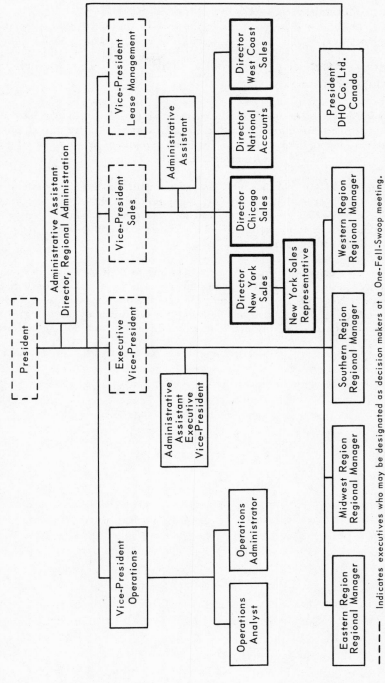

---- Indicates executives who may be designated as decision makers at a One-Fell-Swoop meeting.

—— Indicates the persons responsible for contact and follow-through with prospects for a One-Fell-Swoop meeting.

SALES COORDINATOR'S ROLE

Lee Labita, administrative assistant to Fred LeBouef, vice-president of sales, described her role as coordinator of the One-Fell-Swoop Group operation:

> By screening lists of major U.S. firms, I am able to determine the most probable prospects for our program. I then call a major executive in each of these firms to discuss briefly with him his firm's receptivity to public warehousing in general and to D. H. Overmyer specifically.
>
> Through this initial call I make an appointment for one of our salesmen to talk to their executive in charge of distribution or traffic. After the salesman's visit he submits a report on the call and the prospects for a successful and profitable sale. If the prospects look good at that point, then I set up the One-Fell-Swoop Group meeting.
>
> I set up a group of about five men according to their area of expertise, and subject to their availability. Among them is a decision maker from our head office in New York; he can commit the firm. Before our team meets with the client's team, I brief them on the history of the firm they are going to see—past activities, special considerations in handling their product, and so forth.

5. Materials

MATERIALS are viewed here as products that are processed only in part so that they can be utilized in the production of a final product. Among the materials discussed are synthetic fibers; aluminum and steel bars, sheets, and wire; wheat starch and flour; and processed eggs. Such products are frequently seen as commodities and as such are subject to the problems of commodity selling.

Among the serious challenges facing the producers of materials are these four.

1. *Product differentiation.* Perhaps the greatest challenge among materials manufacturers is that of differentiating their product—to make it appear unique in the eyes of the buyer. The matter of product differentiation is perhaps the sharpest distinction between the sale of materials and the sale of consumer goods, installations, and services. The product that is differentiated can command a higher price and a user franchise: It has an identity all its own, which customers will seek and pay to obtain. The undifferentiated product, on the other hand, has no unique properties that will tie users to repeat sales.

2. *Indirect relationship with both dealer and consumer.* In the companies studied there is no direct contact with the final seller and the final buyer of the product containing the material. Thus not only is the product quite undifferentiated but there is little opportunity for a manufacturer to convince the ultimate users to demand the product by name and thereby pull it through the marketing channels. Even if the consumer could be convinced to request the material by name, he would usually be unable to identify the material in the final form of the product.

3. *Establishing product substitutability.* Another challenge facing materials manufacturers is to convince the materials user that the seller has an acceptable substitute for the materials being used. It is no small task to deliver the message that aluminum can perhaps substitute for steel in many instances, that wheat starch can be substituted for corn starch, and that new synthetic fibers are better than some old synthetic fibers.

The materials salesman may frequently find himself frustrated in trying to deliver his special message beyond those people who look only for low prices on their reorders.

4. *Finding good sales recruits.* The companies studied all were concerned with recruiting and training salesmen who were technically knowledgeable so that they could understand and solve customer problems; creative and imaginative so that they could develop solutions unique to the real nature of the problems and not merely replay old solutions, applicable or not; and of such a nature and character that they could maintain long-term customer relations at high dollar sales volume.

CASE STUDIES

The companies selected for study were Du Pont of Canada Limited (a subsidiary of E. I. du Pont de Nemours & Co.), a major supplier in the Canadian chemicals industry; an aluminum company; a steel company; and The Ogilvie Flour Mills Company, Limited, a major Canadian food producer and a subsidiary of John Labatt, Limited.

MAJOR CONCLUSIONS

Each company sought some form of differentiation, which did not necessarily involve the product per se. Among the techniques used to accomplish this were indirect selling, such as institutional advertising, promotion sequences, and missionary salesmen aimed at the customer's customer; furnishing customers with expert advice on the use of the materials and on the production of the final product; friendly intercompany relations at a number of levels.

Several of the companies that are discussed in this chapter gave direct or indirect financial aid to their customers through extended terms or introduction to their bankers.

Several companies sold or urged customers to purchase specialized machinery that was usable primarily with the seller's materials; this reduced the possibility of loss of the customer to a competitor.

None of the companies sought to make large, one-shot sales, but geared their selling activities to the long-range, large-scale selling and the close, almost daily relations involved in being the primary resource for materials.

Du Pont of Canada

Du Pont has been part of the Canadian chemicals industry for more than a century. Its annual sales exceed $200 million in chemicals, explosives, films, finishes, plastics, textile fibers, and other items. The company's activities are not confined to Canada; rather, they include exports to over 50 countries. A very significant percentage of the company is Canadian-owned.

Sales Sequence

Generally speaking, the management of a major sale in Du Pont fibers comprises three phases.

- *Phase 1: Development selling.* The value of the fiber is explained to the customer.
- *Phase 2: Pyramid selling.* An effort is made to sell a new fiber to the key user in the field; others will then follow.
- *Phase 3: Customer support.* The company helps launch the customer into successful production and sale of the product using the new Du Pont fiber.

Du Pont's Sales Function

Frank McCarthy, vice-president of operations, noted that Du Pont does not engage in single large sales such as an aircraft manufacturer would, but instead is involved in establishing long-lasting, mutually beneficial relations with its customers. The end result for Du Pont is high annual poundage per customer.

D. S. MacKay, Du Pont's fibres group marketing manager, describes the company's role: "Du Pont of Canada largely is a maker and seller of industrial goods which might be classed as basic materials (chemicals or textiles) which only after sale by Du Pont are consumed in end products which may find their way to the ultimate buyer with or without any identification of the 'hidden product' or basic material."

In describing the breadth of the sales function at Du Pont, Mr. MacKay said, "Du Pont salesmen may be found under a variety of labels which are intended to try to describe the function; for example, sales representative, merchandising representative, sales manager, marketing manager, product manager, retail manager, sales development manager, district sales manager, and technical service manager."

With its strong orientation to research, Du Pont has introduced numerous products over the years. Because Du Pont is little involved in producing consumer goods and sells mainly through other producers, a considerable sales effort goes to getting customers to use its new products in their production. Mr. MacKay said, "An important situation in which Du Pont of Canada salesmen are often found is in the product development area of the customers' business, where we try to stimulate the customers to experiment with our basic materials to create new end products. This development period is measured in weeks or more often in months and may involve a number of specialized marketing personnel."

At Du Pont all the selling is done through operating-echelon people. Unlike many other companies, the top executives at Du Pont give virtually no sales help. They will, however, act on problems received from top executives of client companies, but they will not interfere with product divisions' sales efforts. Mr. McCarthy said, "When I happen to meet with a top executive of a client firm, I don't discuss pending orders because I don't know what orders are pending. I don't ask for orders or favors."

Du Pont products, especially hosiery and nylon carpeting, form the major ingredient in the customer's product. As a result the intercompany relationship is very close. Du Pont salesmen will call on the major accounts daily and usually talk to the company president in person on these calls. Close harmony between Du Pont's backup staff and the manufacturer's technical personnel is a necessity. Du Pont recognizes this need and deliberately facilitates a good communications network. Du Pont gets a premium price for its products and feels a very real obligation to justify it.

THE TUFTED CARPET YARN CASE

Tufted carpet yarn has recently broken into the market. The major selling points for a new item stem from the very fact that it is new and therefore differentiated and able to bring a higher price.

A major sale in tufted carpeting is to have a carpet mill producing tufted carpet with Du Pont nylon yarn. The marketing plan used to achieve this goal follows. The organization of the fibres group home furnishings division is shown in Exhibit 17.

EXHIBIT 17. *Organization of Home Furnishings Division, Fibres Group, Du Pont (Canada)*

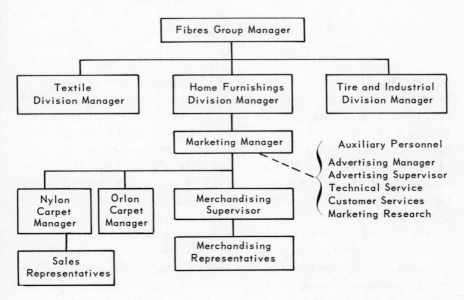

Phase 1: Development selling. Following the development and testing of the product, Du Pont mobilized an effort to convince customers that tufted nylon carpeting was good business. The company conducted market research to determine sales potential for the carpet, the attitude of consumers and retailers, and the acceptability of the *501* trademark.

The results of the research, all of which were positive, were conveyed to carpet manufacturers.

Phase 2: Pyramid selling. Since the carpet manufacturers did not have the carpet-making machinery to tuft nylon, Du Pont concentrated sales efforts on one prime, high-quality, highly respected manufacturer and sold him on the idea of entering into the tufted nylon carpeting business. Over time, Du Pont felt, the other manufacturers would then make the same decision; within ten years all were figured to join in. Building a customer list is similar to working one's way down a pyramid.

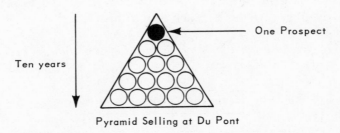

Pyramid Selling at Du Pont

The major contacts at the target manufacturer were the president, the production manager, and the marketing personnel. The effort was to convince them to enter the field and therefore to buy the necessary machinery. To do this Du Pont had to be prepared to assist in contacts and technical discussions with suppliers, set up a pilot plant to tuft carpeting and make this facility available for customers to see, and help the customer decide on correct equipment for his size and market. Sometimes this equipment investment might be as high as $100,000.

Phase 3: Customer support. After the prospect had agreed to enter the tufted nylon carpet business, Du Pont began to launch the company successfully into the new line by helping the carpet maker develop styles and designs; teaching his technical people to process the yarn properly; and developing a good advertising and promotional package that included home shows, TV programs, advertising campaigns, and retail sales training.

THE HOSIERY YARN CASE

Hosiery yarn is an old item that over time has been copied by competitors, and can better be described as a commodity than as a product. The real sales task in hosiery yarn is to sell it successfully in a competitive and declining price market.

The hosiery yarn department is a profit center in itself, and is part of the textile division in the fibres group (See Exhibit 18). The selling

EXHIBIT 18. *Organization of Hosiery Yarn Department, Fibres Group, Du Pont (Canada)*

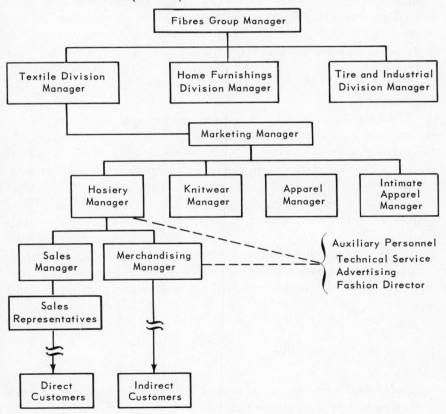

effort in hosiery yarn comprises two categories: (1) direct customers (hosiery mills); this activity is under the jurisdiction of the sales manager for hosiery, and (2) indirect customers (retail women's wear stores); the merchandising manager for hosiery sees that customers are contacted, sales developed, and promotions run.

The merchandising manager for hosiery has an additional function: He coordinates and supervises the activities of auxiliary people serving the hosiery profit center—the technical service personnel, advertising staff, and fashion director.

A major sale in the hosiery department is to bring about a relationship in which a direct customer accepts Du Pont hosiery yarn on a continuing-delivery basis. Du Pont had accomplished this successfully for years in its hosiery yarn business, but other companies, foreign and domestic, entered the field and made a commodity of the yarn and drove the price down significantly. Despite the large number of pounds Du Pont sold annually, profit became increasingly more difficult. Therefore Du Pont recycled the product life of hosiery yarn by introducing a new yarn, Cantrece stretch yarn. This is a premium product with new and distinctive qualities, which enabled both Du Pont and the hosiery mills to upgrade quality and price on the basis of value in use.

The introduction of Cantrece required a total marketing effort. In addition to the efforts of both the sales and the merchandising staffs, Du Pont had to back them up with quality in the product, service to the customer, prompt delivery as scheduled, good technical service for the direct users, and the Du Pont trademark. (See Exhibit 19.) All this was necessary if the product was to be seen as something besides a commodity and thereby bring a higher price per pound to Du Pont.

In effect, Du Pont in the introduction of Cantrece sought to utilize the three-phase marketing it used in such items as *501* tufted carpet yarn: development selling, pyramid selling, and customer support.

An Aluminum Company

The company is a manufacturer of bar, wire, and sheets of aluminum, which it sells to companies that then process it into products.

The company's sales organization is designed to serve its four major markets: industrial, packaging, architectural, and consumer.

SALES SEQUENCE

The major sale at this company can be described broadly as comprising four steps:

1. Create a unique sales force, one that is developed to sell aluminum rather than more traditional materials.

EXHIBIT 19. *Total Marketing Effort, Du Pont (Canada)*

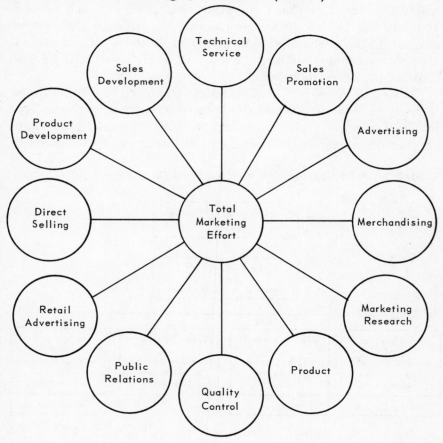

2. Train the salesman to get beyond the purchasing agent.
3. Utilize total corporate effort in supporting the salesman's effort.
4. Utilize the headquarters sales presentation, if necessary.

Because of the relative newness of aluminum as an industrial metal, and the type of selling this newness requires, the company had to evolve these steps as original concepts, which will be described later. When these concepts are viewed together as an interrelated whole, they describe the company's way of managing the sale.

SALES ORGANIZATION

Each regional sales office is divided quite similarly to the four major divisions at headquarters (industrial, packaging, architectural, and consumer). This discussion concentrates principally on the industrial division, which includes the defense, machinery, chemicals, foundry, consumer durable, and transportation industries. The organization is shown in Exhibit 20.

The company uses a "major account" approach to the aluminum industry, in that its salesman concentrates on those accounts that purchase or could purchase upward of $100,000 annually. Accounts are classified at regional offices into the following categories: accounts

EXHIBIT 20. *Sales Organization, an Aluminum Company*

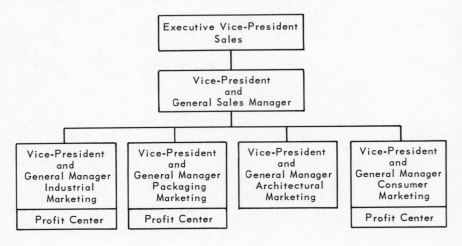

purchasing $100,000 from the company; accounts purchasing $100,-000 annually in products the company makes, but not purchasing all from the company; accounts purchasing $100,000 annually in products the company makes, but purchasing nothing from the company itself; accounts with a potential of $100,000 in purchases, but buying almost nothing from the company (for example, a company using steel or wood instead of aluminum); and distributors. Each salesman usually has a balance of the first four types of account, but spends 70 percent of his time on the first type.

CREATING A UNIQUE SALES FORCE

A major contributor to the company's success has been its concept of selling and marketing. Company executives have learned that success in selling aluminum requires that they create their own salesmen —not obtain them elsewhere. An executive explained it this way:

> The salesmen that competitors lose are frequently the ones they want to lose anyway. Stealing a salesman saves his old employer the trouble of firing him. To add to the incongruity of the matter, his new employer gives him an even higher salary.
>
> Salesmen elsewhere have been trained differently from what we want. Selling aluminum requires a quite different mode of selling. Since the product is so new, its full potential has only begun to be tapped. Therefore, aluminum needs men with conceptual skill—the ability to see old things in new ways—and real creativity so that new uses and ideas can be developed for aluminum.
>
> Our salesmen must get customers to think "aluminum" and design products to utilize aluminum. Hard-sell, arm-twisting salesmen haven't gotten anything but initial orders if the customers don't think aluminum.

The executive offered an example of "thinking aluminum": Because galvanized steel roofing was 24 inches wide, aluminum roofing was also made 24 inches wide. It was later realized that steel had chosen that width because of the weight and the roofers' inability to work effectively with a larger, therefore heavier, piece of steel. Aluminum therefore began making 48-inch and 52-inch widths, thus making the job easier and faster for roofers."

The company has, in effect, redefined what it sells. Although in fact it ships sheets, bars, and wire, its salesmen are selling a whole service and a better way of doing things. The executive likened the whole redefinition to the story of the drill salesman who claimed that he didn't sell cheap drills, but rather sold cheap holes.

Because of the company's strong belief in creating rather than buying salesmen, it has developed a rigorous training program. It takes at least two years to develop a good starting salesman who has the necessary understanding of aluminum. This is a long training period for a salesman who has been successful elsewhere.

Alternate Sources of Salesmen and Their Development Routes
in an Aluminum Company

A	*B*
Men with business experience, perhaps outside the company; age: 26 to 30.	Field trainee fresh from college.
1. HQ trainee as administrative assistant getting 9 to 12 months of broad experience.	1. Sales trainee as inside salesman for 12 to 18 months. Closely observed for promotability.
2. Industrial sales training, which takes two months.	2. At this point the trainee can choose between following the administrative path (No. 3, below) or continuing his sales training (No. 2, left).
3. Starting salesman.	3. Administrative route.
4. Salesman with experience.	
5. Senior salesman.	

Getting Past the Purchasing Agent

Unlike many companies that attempt to bypass the purchasing agent (PA) after the first call, the company's men work continuously with him. This practice continues even if the PA is obviously a rubber stamp. The PA can suggest and recommend or influence his superiors; he can be a good source of information to the salesmen in that he knows the informal power structure and individual behavior patterns within the structure.

However, if the salesman remains tied only to the PA, he will be but a bidder for the client's purchases as the company's needs are communicated to the PA. If the salesman is to be successful, he must become involved with the customer's upper-echelon decision makers. The sale of aluminum, more than most other products, requires high-level selling to overcome the traditional mind-set favoring steel or wood. The aluminum salesman must get beyond the PA. How? An executive answered that by saying, "By hiring good men, and training them to want to get beyond the PA in order to be successful! If he realizes that he must get past the PA in order to succeed, then he will impose his intellectual capacity to the task."

Moving beyond the PA can usually be done by a simple device many salesmen overlook: enlisting the PA's advice and assistance in an honest and straightforward manner. If properly dealt with, the PA soon realizes that the salesman is a problem solver, and so will put him in touch with the people who are having the problems.

UTILIZING THE TOTAL CORPORATE EFFORT

Total corporate effort means just that when it comes to producing sales. The full effort of the company should be utilized as needed in helping to make the sale. Everyone should be available to help— everyone, including researchers, executives, production experts.

After the salesman has made contact with the upper echelons of the prospect company, he begins looking for problems to solve. Getting involved in the solution of the customer's problems helps the salesman to demonstrate his effectiveness and value to the client company so that it will regard him as increasingly necessary to its own problem solving and planning, and to sell what he is paid to sell, because the client wants and needs the products, not because he feels obligated to buy them.

If the salesman is well versed on how to muster the unified efforts of his company, he is in a better position to be of valuable service to his customers—and in a better position to organize the customer's unified effort when his own company is engaged in purchasing products from the prospect company.

HEADQUARTERS SALES PRESENTATIONS

Closely allied with total corporate effort is the headquarters sales presentation, a full-scale, high-level conference including company and customer executives. The presentation is used in two ways: (1) to introduce a new development to a major potential user or (2) to present the company's solution to a significant problem for which the customer has sought its help.

A special auditorium has been designed for effective presentations for as few as four or five or as many as a hundred people. The company has a drama coach to train its sales and engineering personnel in public speaking and effective presentation.

Customer executives are flown to the presentation in a company plane the evening before the presentation; they have dinner and informal talks with company executives. The next day, at the auditorium, the customer executives are given a staged presentation especially prepared for them:

- A special professional announcer.
- Special films or commercials showing the products.
- A special printed program listing the events for the day and a list of those present and their titles.
- The product that the customer is being shown, complete with his own trademarks.

The purpose is more than merely creating a favorable impression on the visitors; the real purpose is to demonstrate to the customer the end product that he could produce with company help and the total corporate effort.

While aluminum is a unique metal, it is still a commodity among competing aluminum manufacturers. The company's concept of selling aluminum helps give the product identity and raise it above parity-price competition in the marketplace.

A STEEL COMPANY

In direct contrast with the aluminum company's approach, the steel company that is the subject of this case study has learned to exercise considerable caution in helping its customers solve problems. When the steel company's R&D staff discover a new process believed to be beneficial to its customers, they are likely to recall the experience of a major competitor. The competitor had held an elaborate presentation to announce the news of a new process for its customers. At the conclusion of the presentation, however, customer executives asked their R&D people, also in attendance, why they had not thought of it first since that was, after all, what they were paid to do. The R&D people were angry and embarrassed at being shown up as "asleep at the switch." The competitor steel company, despite its good intentions, found itself the focus of some hard feelings.

The steel company has a number of major divisions that work in concert through company headquarters.

SALES SEQUENCE

The sequence in managing a major sale of steel is organized into three steps, each performed by a specialized group:

1. The major selling tool is the corporate sales force, which obtains and maintains a close relationship with clients.
2. When required by the corporate sales force, the divisional staff people furnish backup support.
3. As large sales develop, the executive sales staff backs up the sales force and the sales staff until the order is completed.

THE SALES TEAM

The sales effort is organized under the vice-president, sales, who in turn works with the vice-president, sales, of each of the divisions. The relationship of these executives concerns only sales policy, sales strategy, pricing, and advice and information. There is no line authority from the vice-president, sales, to the divisional sales vice-presidents; each of the divisional sales vice-presidents is under the line authority of the division president.

The sales team comprises three complementary groups that work in close harmony:

1. The headquarters sales force, the main selling tool.
2. The sales staffs from each division, which furnish backup support for the headquarters sales force. Each of the divisional sales staffs is composed of the following divisional people: president; vice-president, sales; production manager plus staff; customer service manager plus expediters and inventory personnel; quality control manager plus staff; technical service manager plus staff; and product and market development manager plus staff, including research.
3. The executive sales staff, a combination of about a dozen top executives who back up the divisional sales staffs and the headquarters sales force.

The headquarters sales force. Many of the salesmen on the headquarters sales force know steel from mill experience. This was emphasized by a company executive:

> Many of the sales force and divisional sales staff are men whose fathers were immigrant steel workers and proud of their association with the company. The second-generation men have the same familial feelings about the firm; they are hometown boys making good and a source of great pride to the community. We have no Ivy League types who act pompous and are reluctant to get dirty. . . .
>
> Here we have a sense of camaraderie, unity, and cooperation that produces a very synergic effect. It is quite evident to our customers, and it helps to bring them back again and again. We have been able to achieve a highly personalized involvement and rapport with our customers. Of significant help in doing this is the three-level unity resulting from the close cooperation of the sales force, sales staff, and executive sales staff.

The sales force seeks help from the sales staff as needed; and, depending on the type of help a salesman requires, it is requested directly or through his superior. How much support the salesman is given depends on the size of the potential order involved and the amount of the corporate investment in the support. Over time, a salesman begins to develop an ad hoc group that he calls on repeatedly. Such team effort is used all the time, but care is taken not to inundate the buyer with sales people.

Calls are frequent, however—one to eight times per month, and there may be ten to twenty backup people involved with a major customer at one time. The salesman is kept fully apprised about which other people are dealing with a client at the same time, and exactly what they are doing.

The customer's purchasing agent is the contact—initially and on a continuing basis. (In large accounts, more than 25,000 tons per year, the salesman contacts the president.) Beyond that the salesman sees who the PA wants him to see; after that he is on his own in the company. Steel is a long-term, repeat-sale business, and so the salesman keeps all his contacts alive.

The divisional sales staff is brought into the selling situation by the sales force as needed for help in the sale. The sales staff has experts on products, quality, product and market development, inventory control, research, and technical service—all geared to helping the customer do a better job. Sales staff people are involved in the customer's production facilities, offices, and sales conferences. Sales staff is the technical support the sales force needs in helping solve customer's problems in steel.

The executive sales staff is composed of the vice-president, sales; general manager, executive sales staff; manager of sales administration; manager of commercial research; assistant vice-president, sales, for each geographic region; vice-president, sales, for each company division; and assistant to vice-president, sales.

Executive sales staff members are all sales administrators of one sort or another who direct sales information flow, and who have considerable administrative responsibility. Although executive sales staff members are not salesmen per se, they regard themselves as salesmen in the best traditions. They act as aides to the sales force and not as supersalesmen. As one of these executives commented: "This group is composed of individuals who have a great commitment to the firm in their administrative roles alone, but in addition are heavily involved in highly personalized tasks in aiding the sales force. The job of aiding the sales force is virtually a seven-day task—home weekends and frequently that is all."

The activities of the executive sales staff can be described as follows:

- Work mainly with large accounts but not exclusively so.
- Help maintain a customer relationship they may have gained in their executive-echelon sales force days.
- Help close large sales.

- Maintain close, friendly rapport with customers: family gatherings, sporting events, social get-togethers, entertainment.
- Dig out problems that customers are experiencing.

The staff meets quarterly for a two-day critique session, where they level with one another about the problems customers are having in their dealings with the company. The talk is frank, but the staff are not destructive of one another; discussion might center on such matters as slow delivery, poor quality, lack of coordination in making a sale.

But the unity, cooperation, and team effort on the sales side really don't describe the whole sales picture at this company. A sales executive said:

> As trite as it may sound, it has genuine meaning here when I say that all our people make the difference in our success. And I am including the men in the mill who make the steel, because they literally are part of the selling effort.
>
> The several generations of employees here are proud to be growing with the firm. The sense of upward movement for the family in its relationship with the company produces a sense of unity and spirit that pervades the workers, sales personnel, and company executives. Employees are not stuffy or snobbish but are what they are: good, second-generation, steel people who care about the company and its future.
>
> The workers are notified continuously as to whose order they are filling. Customers are brought frequently into the mill for interviews with various workmen producing their order. The workmen are quite familiar with the customer's likes and dislikes and idiosyncrasies; it is not uncommon for them to comment, "This order is for XYZ, and you know how they like their steel to be."

The Ogilvie Flour Mills Company, Limited

Ogilvie is the food group of the Canadian brewing firm John Labatt, Limited. The combined Labatt organization has operations, investments, and subsidiaries in many nations, including the United States, Europe, and Central and South America. This discussion focuses on three Ogilvie divisions: Industrial Grain Products Limited (starches and chemicals), Food Service Division, and Ogilvie Bakery and Industrial Foods.

SALES SEQUENCE

Managing the major sale in Industrial Grain Products—as an example, converting a corrugating plant to wheat starch—involves the following eight steps:

1. Obtain from production manager his present cornstarch formula and operating conditions.
2. On the basis of the information from the production manager, the technical service department develops a wheat starch formula and procedure suitable for the specific plant conditions.
3. Present the proposed new formula and procedures to prospect for evaluation.
4. Schedule a trial run for adjustment of formula, production of a few batches, and a short corrugating run (part day) on a grade requiring the least quality control at the prospect's plant.
5. Schedule a minimum two-week run on results of trial run.
6. Technical representative spends about one week at customer's plant adapting formulations to different grades of corrugating board. Samples of board are taken by customer and the technical representative for further testing in laboratories. Customer then continues balance of run with Industrial Grain Products personnel.
7. After all tests are evaluated and wheat starch accepted as a competitive product, sales representative negotiates share of business and delivery patterns.
8. Technical representative makes periodic calls to check on performance.

In the two other divisions, Ogilvie Bakery and Industrial Foods and Food Service, the study concentrated on repeat sales, or continuing large sales, to major customers. The continuing-sale process is more varied and lends itself less easily to summarization.

FUNCTIONS OF THE DIVISIONS

Industrial Grain Products produces wheat starch for industrial use by the textile and paper industries, adhesive manufacturers, and food and chemical processors. This division also produces vital and devitalized gluten for increasing the protein and baking characteristics of flour and other foods and hydrolysates, which are used as flavoring agents in soups, sauces, and specialty foods.

The Food Service Division, in operation only several years, deals with egg processing, meat processing, hatcheries, and animal feed. In addition, it is engaged in totally vertically integrated feeding operations in restaurants and institutions; the food is processed from the ground or animal to the final frozen portion, which will be served ready to eat.

The Bakery and Industrial Foods Division deals with products sold in bulk to other processors or manufacturers. These include Ogilvie bakery flour, sold in Canada and abroad; no grain or flour may be sold to the United States.

THE SALE OF WHEAT STARCH

Industrial Grain Products Limited (IGP), Ogilvie's starches and chemicals division, is caught perennially in the problem of balancing its sales between starch and gluten, the two major components of the wheat kernel. The current effort is to increase starch sales to keep in balance with gluten sales. Wheat starch has wide usage; for example, paper coatings, corrugating and other adhesives, core binding for foundries, textile warp sizing, gypsum board, wallpaper paste, oil drilling muds, flotation in potash mining, explosives, laundry starch, pharmaceuticals, brewing and distilling, baking powder, and icing sugar.

However, since the pulp and paper industry represents approximately 50 percent of the starch market, it must be the prime target. "But," said Nick Kalin, at the time of this study marketing manager at IGP, now vice-president and general manager, "if that's our obvious target, then it's also the obvious target for our competitors. That means that we have to find a better way to sell it and hopefully remove it from a price-competitive commodity classification. We must do a better job—and adapt readily to the changing demands of this industry."

The Industrial Grain Products sales representative sees the purchasing agent. In the case of calls in the paper industry, the PA will send the representative to the technical supervisor or the production

EXHIBIT 21. *Sales Organization Structure, Industrial Grain Products Division, Ogilvie Flour Mills*

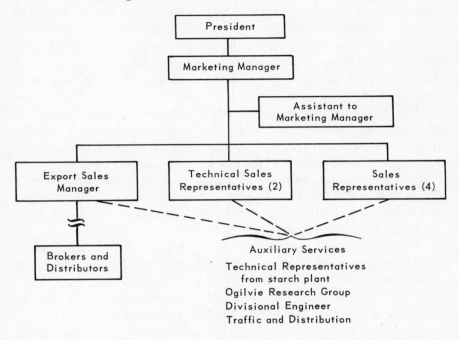

manager, who is in charge of the end-use application of starch. The plant manager will become involved by the time a trial of the starch is offered. (Exhibit 21 shows IGP's sales organization.)

A major wheat starch sale is having the customer use IGP's wheat starch on a regular basis in the production of corrugated paper. There are eight steps in managing the sale.

1. After meeting with the PA and the plant superintendent, the salesman obtains from them the current formula (probably corn starch) and operating procedure.

2. The salesman gives the formula to Ogilvie R&D and has the staff create a new formula based on wheat starch. R&D tests the new formula in its own plant and obtains samples and data on costs, strengths, viscosity, and so forth.

3. The salesman presents the new formula, samples, and data to the prospect for observation and testing.

4. A trial run is scheduled with the customer's adhesive manager

in its plant; IGP brings its sales representative, technical representative, and other auxiliary help as required. Finalizing the formula takes about one week of trials. The customer pays for all the ingredients in those batches that produce usable products.

5. If the tests have thus far proved successful, the customer then orders a trial shipment of wheat starch, which he will then use with only his people present. This is a crucial time for IGP, as none of its personnel will be present.

The adhesive manager is the key individual during this week of trial, as he can make or break the results if he so desires. The seller treats him cordially and with due respect. Too much attention to the adhesive manager puts him in an embarrassing position and can bring the resentment of his superior, who can veto the purchase even if the tests are good. Conversely, special treatment of the superior can bring the resentment of the adhesive manager—especially if the superior urges him to buy the product.

Mr. Kalin said, "We do not believe in buying their business, no special gifts, nothing. However, if circumstances warrant, we may ask those concerned to have lunch or dinner with us."

6. During the trial run, which may at times go several weeks, we follow up on problems as they occur; 75 percent of the problems are not the result of our product or formula, but stem from factory problems such as bacteria, human error, the need for equipment adjustment, or a lack of cleanliness.

"We are no longer starch salesmen," Mr. Kalin said; "we are now sending our men to school to learn more about corrugating equipment and plant operations. They must virtually be experts on running a corrugating plant because operating personnel frequently are not adequately knowledgeable in overall equipment adjustment, variations of material, sensitivity of the formula, and adjustments to the formula to adapt to [these] variations."

7. If all goes well, wheat starch is accepted as a usable product. The customer must then be sold on the maximum use of wheat starch in his corrugated board production. Confidence in IGP technical skills has a large bearing on this decision.

8. The salesman contacts the client regularly and, depending on the amount of starch used, will see him on a three- to nine-week cycle

of calls. Meanwhile, an IGP technical representative is in frequent contact with the customer during the early stages and sets up periodic follow-up calls.

The "Thermal Mechanical Converter" Sale

Mr. Kalin pointed out that Industrial Grain Products recently commenced marketing a new starch converter the company had developed. The machine converts raw (pearl) starch mechanically and thermally on the job; the quality of the starch processed by the converter is equivalent to that of the more expensive chemically treated starch. The customer saves by buying a cheaper grade of starch and also by extending the use of the starch.

With this new machine and the special arrangements that go with its use, IGP is able to create close, long-term, mutually profitable relationships with its customers. It is an interesting solution to the problem of selling commodities.

The machine is installed in the customer's plant with these arrangements:

1. The machine is either sold or leased to the customer.
2. IGP provides engineering design and installation and start-up assistance for the converter. A percentage of the client's starch purchases for a period of five years is usually negotiated.
3. IGP provides the technical service to keep the machine operating effectively.

A brief description of the sales pattern follows.

1. The salesman contacts the prospect, gives his presentation, and leaves the necessary printed materials. He offers to provide at cost sufficient converted and dried sample product for testing.

2. The technical representatives goes to the prospective client with the salesman to make a feasibility study and prepare a report on his findings.

3. IGP's divisional engineer evaluates the feasibility study and designs a starch converter and suitable layout to fit into the plant.

4. The salesman makes the proposal to the prospect; in addition,

he gives the prospect a guarantee on minimum savings that can be achieved with the converter.

5. If the proposal is accepted, IGP personnel supervise the installation of the equipment, and the customer's personnel are trained to operate the unit. IGP personnel run the equipment for one week and observe closely for a second week as the customer's employees operate it.

6. IGP stays in close contact with the customer, and regular follow-up calls are maintained to insure adequate performance of the converting unit.

In the Industrial Grain Products Division the effort to make large sales will rarely go much higher up the line than to the marketing manager. In the case of a particularly large sale, G. J. Dunne (IGP president) and other Ogilvie officials may enter the scene.

THE FOOD SERVICE DIVISION AND THE SALE OF EGGS

[The Food Service Division at Ogilvie has now been merged into the Bakery and Industrial Foods Division. The information presented in this case reflects the situation before the merger.—Ed.]

The Food Service Division at Ogilvie is the major processor in the Canadian egg market. Just as the starch and chemical division is under pressure to balance its sales of starch and gluten, Food Service must balance its sales of whites and yolks. The yolks are sold principally to food manufacturers for the production of mayonnaise and similar products; the whites are sold principally to bakers and cake mix and candy manufacturers. Currently, egg whites are in greater supply than yolks.

H. J. Mulhaner, president of the Food Service Division, described the selling process and the nature of the relationship between his division and a large processed-egg customer in the grocery manufacturing industry.

Of particular interest in the sale of eggs described here is the nature of the intercompany relationship and the high degree of involvement and interdependence. This closely structured relationship between the buyer and the seller was not found in any other company studied. The relationship between the Food Service Division and the large processed-egg customer is noteworthy because it is unlike ordinary buyer–seller relationships. The customer's behavior is typical of many large manufacturers of advertised-label products. To insure the continuity of supply of its materials, to prevent any variance in its product's quality, and to stabilize the prices it pays for materials, the customer engages in several practices:

- Sets its own specifications for the eggs it will buy.
- Regularly inspects its suppliers' plants.
- Must approve the plants before considering the addition of an egg supplier.
- Maintains a list of approved egg-processing plants even if it does not buy from them.
- Buys eggs on a fixed-price, six-month contract; contracts are signed about three or four months before they take effect. Thus the supplier must predict a price for eggs nine or ten months in advance.

The Food Service Division is quite capable of operating profitably and giving its customers such added services because of its own expertise in the egg market. The division's external and internal experts advise the company as well as its major customers on market conditions. The experts include an international procurement expert who travels and studies the world market, especially in the United States, China, Poland, and Australia, which are major supply areas, and a father–son team of experts on egg procurement and major egg users.

These three experts make market predictions, which are then passed on to major customers. The major customers usually agree to follow the experts' advice, and contracts are concluded. The market is subject to unpredictable variables such as weather, changes in supply or demand, bad information built into the original prediction. These are risks the manufacturer prefers to avoid and so transfers them all to the Food Service Division through six-month contracts. If predictions are good, Food Service profits; if predictions are poor, Food Service loses.

The intercompany relationship between Ogilvie Mills and the large processed-egg customer is summarized as follows.

Ogilvie	Frequency of Contacts	Contact at Client Company
President, Ogilvie Flour Mills Company, Limited	Occasionally	President
President, Food Service Division	Occasionally, not alone	President Vice-President, Production
General Manager, Food Service Division	Occasionally, not alone	President Vice-President, Production
General Manager, eggs	Regularly, alone	President Vice-President, Production
Special sales representative	Regularly, alone	President Vice-President, Production
Regular salesman	Semimonthly	Purchasing agent

The Food Service Division maintains excellent communication at all levels with the customer. Inventory is checked frequently, and the use rate is noted and subsequent shipments adjusted accordingly.

The degree of involvement of both the buyer and the seller in each other's operations is considerable but is absolutely necessary to both companies. The buyer is able to obtain what he needs when he needs it and at a price he knows in advance; the seller is giving this service as a means of maintaining a long-term relationship. Eggs are a commodity, but eggs with added service are no longer a commodity; they are a differentiated product that justifies customer loyalty.

The Bakery and Industrial Foods Division and the Sale of Flour

The Bakery and Industrial Foods Division is engaged principally in the sale of flour in Canada to commercial bakeries and to baking divisions of grocery chains, and in the export market to its established agents overseas and direct to a major socialist state. The sales organization of the division is shown in Exhibit 22.

EXHIBIT 22. *Sales Organization, Bakery and Industrial Foods Division, Ogilvie Flour Mills*

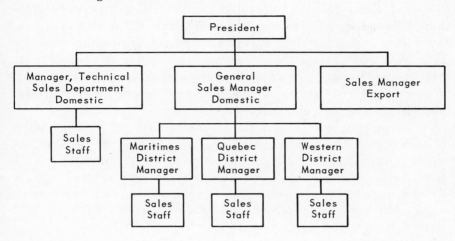

Large domestic sales for the Bakery and Industrial Foods Division consist principally of obtaining reorders from regular customers since the company already sells to virtually all the major buyers, and is well represented among small and medium users.

John F. Blakney, president, described a typical relationship with a large bakery customer in terms of who contacts whom—

Bakery and Industrial Foods Division	*Frequency of Contacts*	*Contact at a Large Bakery*
President	Four times yearly	President
	Occasionally	Purchasing agent
	Occasionally	Local plant manager
General sales manager	Monthly	Executives, including purchasing agent
	Occasionally	Local plant manager
District sales manager	Weekly	Local plant manager
	Occasionally	Purchasing agent
Salesman	Weekly	Manager of small plant or branch of a multiple operation

The Domestic Market for Industrial Flour

Mr. Blakney described the various large domestic users of industrial flour as belonging to two major categories: controlled and noncontrolled. He said, "The controlled accounts may be either actually controlled by a major milling company, or else tied to a major milling company by reason of a loan. In either case the account is certainly not going to buy from anyone else. The 'tied' account is found more often in milling, feed, and starch.

"The noncontrolled accounts may actually have a captive supplier—a mill that it owns outright or has a long-term contract with; or the noncontrolled account may be quite free to buy anywhere. The free account generally buys from two or three suppliers and applies leverage to keep the price down. In fact the millers must renegotiate a price with their accounts every 30 to 60 days."

Pattern for Contract Renewal

Industrial flour sales are, for the established company, virtually all repeat sales. Thus the major sale is actually the renewal of flour contracts every 30 to 60 days. Assuming that the shipper has maintained quality, exact service, and in-plant technical service, the usual repeat-order procedure involves five steps.

1. The district sales manager calls on the account weekly to set up the order flow against the contract and to look for problems that might threaten the relationship. This latter is, in effect, maintenance selling. Meanwhile, the president calls on the customer at least four times per year, and the general sales manager calls every month, sometimes with the district sales manager.

2. Every month the general or district sales manager calls the account to quote the price that has been set for the upcoming month.

3. Within a few days the customer calls back and says either that the price is acceptable or that it is unacceptable. If the price is acceptable, the contract is set.

4. If the Bakery and Industrial Foods Division's price is unacceptable, the customer tells the manager how far out of line the price is. The general sales manager has very narrow price confines within which to work, so he may have to confer with the president before going below a predetermined level.

5. If both companies can reach an agreement on the price, the customer approves and the contract is set.

THE ROLE OF PRICE

The question of price in industrial flour sales is ever present but is not the single major factor in customer purchase decisions. In essence, the buyers want to feel that they are buying fairly—that is, not paying more than their competition. The buyers also hesitate to change flours because it may change their baking formulas somewhat. The result is that, if a miller's price is higher than the price others are offering, the customer may well tell him how much to come down.

Mr. Blakney pointed out that the customer would never say the company was 10 cents too high when it was really 5 cents too high. He explained: "He would say 5 cents if it were 5 cents; he would add nothing. In fact, he might call me long distance at his expense to tell me about the 5 cents."

With but a few major suppliers of flour in the domestic market, the seller behavior follows the typical oligopolistic pattern of following all price cuts. Price reductions to any one customer in fact are automatically extended to all existing customers in the trading area. This can be an extremely costly matter and serves to deter decisions to cut prices when the few pennies per hundred weight are multiplied.

"Accounts are lost," Mr. Blakney said, "not through price necessarily but through faulty service, bad flour, change of personnel, and lack of uniformity. Those are the things that can kill you. Accounts are gained not through price but through innovation, differentiation, solution of the prospect's flour problems, and solution of his nonflour shop problems such as shortening his dough time and increasing his yield."

FUNCTION OF THE TECHNICAL SALES DEPARTMENT

The technical sales department is designed to back up the sales staff in obtaining and retaining accounts. Its main functions are to give in-plant technical advice to customers and to serve as a bridge between the Bakery and Industrial Foods Division's production men and the customer's production men.

The department does not make regular calls on customers, but is called in by the Bakery and Industrial Foods Division's sales people and by the customer's production people. If the department has developed something of interest to some of the customers, it will make field visits on its own authority.

All department members can bake and so are able to understand customer problems and needs. The department tailors flour especially to the customer's needs, which is beneficial to all concerned as it helps to move the flour out of the commodity category and to establish close long-term relationships between the company and its customers. In its dealing with both the company and the customer, the department has considerable freedom and maintains a high degree of objectivity. It has full use of Ogilvie's quality control and research and development laboratories in the performance of its task.

As a backup tool or resource for the sales and production functions at the Bakery and Industrial Foods Division, the technical sales department is invaluable. This is the kind of nonprice activity that Mr. Blakney views as to important in gaining and retaining valued customers.

FUNCTION OF THE EXPORT SALES DEPARTMENT

Somewhat apart from the normal sales operations that are managed by the sales department and the technical sales department is the export department. The export department's regular functions consist of managing its trade with the United Kingdom, Caribbean countries, and West Africa. Canadian wheat, because of its excellent quality, has long had high acceptability; therefore Ogilvie has long-established agents abroad. The agents act as full-service wholesalers, but represent the Bakery and Industrial Foods Division on an exclusive basis.

FLOUR SALES TO A SOCIALIST STATE

A separate but extremely important function of the export sales department is its special sale of flour to a large socialist state. Because of the importance of the sale, Mr. Blakney takes an extremely active personal role. He described the process.

The trading agency of the socialist state fixes, in its capital, a quantity of wheat it seeks to buy in Canada for the coming year. The trading agency then meets with the Canadian Wheat Board and establishes the price. After the price is set, the agency tells the Board how many bushels of the wheat contracted for are to be in flour.

On receiving the information as to how many bushels of wheat are to be milled into flour, the Canadian Wheat Board notifies a consortium of major Canadian-owned flour mills and asks them to contact the trading agency direct. Although the wheat price is set, the Canadian flour group must negotiate for additional money to cover flour bags, milling costs, transportation to the docks, and profit.

The milling industry committee then meets to negotiate with the trading agency either in Canada or in the capital of the socialist state. The trading agency usually designates where the negotiations are to be held.

The whole process of negotiating may take four solid days of very hard work. The buying team is well versed in its task. Its members are hard traders, very patient, and all business.

When the contract is signed, the flour is produced and delivered to Canadian dockside according to the agreed-on schedule. The flour is shipped only in ships belonging to the socialist state, and dockside delivery is coordinated with the availability of their ships. Immediately after the loading is completed and the documentation fixed, the money is paid promptly on the spot without delay.

While it might be cheaper ordinarily for the socialist state to mill its own flour from the wheat it has purchased, it orders it milled in Canada because of the destination—Cuba. Cuba has no significant milling capacity and to mill it anywhere but in Cuba or Canada would entail double handling and shipping costs.

Mr. Blakney, who has been part of the milling committee negotiating team for a number of years, said, "Negotiations are strictly business on both sides. After-hours relations are very cordial; and, if we are negotiating in their country, we are well entertained and well treated. When they come here, we of course extend the same hospitability.

"But what is of more importance," he said, "is the nature of the agreement. It is a very solid contract, very honorable; they never back away. They honor it at 101 percent."

WILLIAM H. KAVEN teaches economics and marketing at the School of Hotel Administration, Cornell University.

He was a wholesaler in Canton, Ohio, for 16 years following his service in WWII. During his years in Canton he was active in state and national trade organizations, city politics, education, service clubs, fund drives, and youth organizations.

In 1962 he sold the firm to employees and moved with his family to Cornell University to complete doctoral studies in administration, marketing, and managerial economics. He received his Ph.D. in 1965. Before returning to Cornell to teach, he taught at Ithaca College, the University of Virginia, and Sir George Williams University (Montreal).

He has served as consultant to the National Food Marketing Commission, the Virginia Employment Commission, and a number of companies in the food industry in the United States and Canada. He is currently directing a series of management training programs for the Norfolk Naval Shipyard.

Dr. Kaven has authored a number of articles in marketing and management journals, and is currently at work on another book.